Penguin Critical Studies

KT-495-181

Tess of the d'Urbervilles

Dr Graham Handley has taught and lectured for more than thirty-five years. He was Principal Lecturer and Head of the English Department at the College of All Saints, Tottenham, and Research Officer in English at Birkbeck College, University of London. He is a part-time lecturer in literature with the University of London Department of Extramural Studies. He has examined at all levels up to and including university honours degree, and has published on Dickens, Mrs Gaskell, George Eliot and Trollope. He has edited *The Mill on the Floss* and *Wuthering Heights* for Macmillan, *Daniel Deronda* and Trollope's *The Three Clerks* for Oxford, and has just completed two books on George Eliot, *The State of the Art: George Eliot* and *The Present Past: George Eliot and the Midlands*. He has written studies of *To Kill a Mockingbird*, *The Pardoner's Tale*, *The Go-Between*, *The Death of Grass*, *Far from the Madding Crowd* and *Look Back in Anger* for the Penguin Passnotes series, and of *Vanity Fair* and *Barchester Towers* for the Penguin Master-studies series.

121 033

Penguin Critical Studies
Advisory Editor: Bryan Loughrey

Thomas Hardy

Tess of the d'Urbervilles

Graham Handley

NORWICH CITY COLLEGE LIBRARY		
Stock No.	121033	
Class	823·9 |HAR	
Cat.	Proc.	

Penguin Books

PENGUIN BOOKS

Published by the Penguin Group
Penguin Books Ltd, 27 Wrights Lane, London W8 5TZ, England
Penguin Books USA Inc., 375 Hudson Street, New York, New York 10014, USA
Penguin Books Australia Ltd, Ringwood, Victoria, Australia
Penguin Books Canada Ltd, 10 Alcorn Avenue, Toronto, Ontario, Canada M4V 3B2
Penguin Books (NZ) Ltd, 182–190 Wairau Road, Auckland 10, New Zealand

Penguin Books Ltd, Registered Offices: Harmondsworth, Middlesex, England

First published 1991
10 9 8 7 6 5 4 3 2

Copyright © Graham Handley, 1991
All rights reserved

The moral right of the author has been asserted

Printed in England by Clays Ltd, St Ives plc
Set in 9/11 pt Monophoto Times

Except in the United States of America, this book is sold subject
to the condition that it shall not, by way of trade or otherwise, be lent,
re-sold, hired out, or otherwise circulated without the publisher's
prior consent in any form of binding or cover other than that in
which it is published and without a similar condition including this
condition being imposed on the subsequent purchaser

For Chelsey, with love

Contents

Acknowledgements

I wish to thank Anne Dangerfield, Janet Hill and Esther Sidwell for help with this study, as well as the generations of critics whose concerns with *Tess of the d'Urbervilles* have made me examine and re-examine my own responses to the novel.

NOTE: All quotations are taken from the Penguin Classics edition of *Tess of the d'Urbervilles* with an introduction by A. Alvarez and edited by David Skilton. Page references in the text are to that edition, but I have also used the Clarendon edition of *Tess of the d'Urbervilles*, ed. Juliet Grindle and Simon Gatrell (1983).

Introduction

Near the end of June 1887 Hardy signed a contract to write a novel which would be about the same length as that of his previous published full-scale work, *The Woodlanders*. The contract was with Tillotson's of Bolton, a firm which published popular serial fiction, and the arrangement was that Hardy would deliver four instalments of the work by the middle of 1889. Apparently he was slow in starting, but by 7 February 1889 he was so firmly committed to the novel that he told Tillotson that he could not undertake 'anything else with safety'. In July he suggested that the title of the novel might be 'The Body and Soul of Sue' (one of Tess's pre-names), though three weeks later this was changed to 'Too Late, Beloved'. The first parts of the novel were sent to the publisher in September.

The search for a title continued to concern Hardy. At one stage he considered *A Daughter of the d'Urbervilles*, which emphasizes the hereditary theme in the novel. This was further stressed in a letter where Hardy says that his heroine is 'a lineal descendant of one of the oldest county families in England', adding 'I should say that her position is based on fact.' But with half of *Too Late Beloved* (without a comma) before them in proof, Tillotson's discovered that what they had agreed to publish did not fit in with their own moral and religious tone. Hardy, asked to revise, recast and bowdlerize, refused; the contract was cancelled, the manuscript returned to the author, and Tillotson's honoured their payment to him. Although in earlier novels, and in the recently published *The Woodlanders*, Hardy had compromised and cut, this novel was different. Not only was it personally, almost intimately felt, but his own attitudes had hardened. It seems that his involvement with his incomplete novel was greater than it might have been had the work been finished.

He began to offer the novel to other magazines. The editor of one of these, Mowbray Morris of *Macmillan's*, offered Hardy a detailed critique in his rejection. He praised the 'rural scenes' and even allowed, in a surprisingly enlightened way, that the 'amateur baptism might perhaps startle some good souls; but there is nothing that can in reason be called irreverent, for poor Tess was obviously in very sober earnestness'. He felt though that there was 'rather too much succulence', and he made specific comments on Hardy's style, finding the thought

1

and the language of the story unclear in parts. It was too 'entirely modern' in conception. This was clearly not a term of praise.

Hardy meanwhile pressed the possibility of publication in the *Graphic*, another popular magazine. He sent in half the novel on 8 October 1890, and the rest before the end of the month. Keenly alive to the repressive and intolerant temper of the time and the dead hand which suffocated explicitness, Hardy cut from this first published version, as he knew he would have to, Tess's seduction and the baptism scene. He adjusted the one in which Angel carries the milkmaids across the flooded road: sexual hypocrisy made a wheelbarrow more acceptable than Angel's arms.

There is little doubt that Hardy was galled but determined. In January 1890, scarcely eighteen months before *Tess* began to appear in the *Graphic*, he had published an article in the *New Review* called 'Candour in English Fiction'. In it he praises the great tragedians of Greece and the Elizabethans and Jacobeans, asserting 'They reflected life, revealed life, criticized life.' And he defines what must be practised to secure popular-magazine publication: 'an arbitrary proclamation has gone forth that certain picked commandments of the ten shall be preserved intact – to wit, the first, third and seventh; that the ninth shall be infringed but gingerly; the sixth only as much as necessary; and the remainder as much as you please, in a genteel manner'. This is indicative of his bitterness and frustration. By March 1891 he was 'putting the finishing touches to Tess', but had already decided to make his own point unequivocally. He determined to publish 'The Midnight Baptism', dangerous to the morality of family readers, separately. Meanwhile the novel appeared as scheduled in the *Graphic* in twenty-four weekly instalments from 4 July to 26 December (but not on 11 July and 7 November) 1891. The three-volume edition appeared at the end of November. It differed from the serial version by being divided into seven 'Phases', an alteration from the original six books. Such was the novel's popularity that a fifth (single volume) edition was published in September 1892. This incorporated a number of adjustments to the plot, themes and dialect, but Hardy continued to make alterations in the text up to and including the Wessex edition of 1912, when it reached its definitive form.

Omitted from the *Graphic* version, as I have indicated above, are two episodes of vital importance, and both are central to Hardy's conception and his determination to free himself from the shackles of contemporary hypocrisy. A study of each of them reveals Hardy's sense of structure, and underlines the emotional compulsion which his novel – and more particularly the character and situation of his heroine – exerted upon

2

him. 'The Midnight Baptism' appeared in the *Fortnightly Review* in May 1891, two months before the serial version began. It was provocatively subtitled 'A Study in Christianity'. It occurs in later printed versions of the novel in Chapter XIV, the whole of which was omitted from the *Graphic*. 'The Midnight Baptism' begins with the description of the 'the revolving arms of the painted reaping machine'. The second paragraph is the poignant account of the various creatures who have retreated into the diminishing area of standing wheat. They are victims, put to death by man and machine, and thus a deliberate natural parallel with the heroine-victim of the novel of which they are an integral part. Of course the *Fortnightly* episode does not name Tess; remember that the novel had not yet begun to appear. But a close look at the *Fortnightly* text provides evidence, when it is set beside the version in the novel, of Hardy's scrupulous attention to detail, his polishing and adjusting. For instance, the description in the *Fortnightly* is in the past tense: Tess's movements in the novel are put into the particularized immediacy of the present. This enhances her individuality and the expansions in the novel are integrated into her character, giving her a natural consistency. They show Hardy's structural control. Take, for example, the discussion in the novel between the two field-women about Tess's feeling for her child:

'A little more than persuading had to do wi' the coming o't, I reckon. There were they that heard a sobbing one night last year in The Chase; and it mid ha' gone hard wi' a certain party if folks had come along.'
   'Well, a little more or a little less, 'twere a thousand pities that it should have happened to she, of all others. But 'tis always the comeliest! . . .' (p. 140)

This exchange, absent from the *Fortnightly* episode, is followed in the novel by further paragraphs of sympathetic identification with Tess. In them Hardy, as so often, is giving us her thoughts on her situation. This detail does not occur in the *Fortnightly*, where the narrative arrives quickly and clinically at crisis point:

When she reached home it was to learn to her grief that the baby had been taken ill quite suddenly since the afternoon.

Apart from removing the redundant 'quite', Hardy retained this and the following paragraph ('The baby's offence against society in coming into the world . . .', p. 142) in the novel. They express with considered emphasis Tess's anguish because the child has not been baptized. And, with minor alterations, the narrative in the novel follows that of the *Fortnightly*, even to the extent of the father's refusal to admit the parson to the house. Admittedly, 'sense of respectability' in the early version is replaced by the fictionally necessary 'sense of the antique nobility of his family'. This is Hardy crafting, integrating meticulously, for by this time we know Sir John well. The vagaries of his moods, particularly when he has been drinking, fully account for his action, but in the *Fortnightly* Hardy appears anxious to get to his subject – the baptism. Broadly, magazine and novel cohere in this major sequence. Typically, though, Hardy adds in the novel, after the description of the arch-fiend and his three-pronged fork, the phrase 'sometimes taught the young in this Christian country'. This personal note, an omniscient bias which is part of the ironic and moral texture of the novel, conveys that depth of feeling which is one of the great strengths of *Tess*. The 'Sissy' of the episode is twice retained in the novel version, and once Hardy subtly amends on emphasis in plain speech: in the morning when they had woken up the children 'begged Sissy to have another pretty baby', but the *Fortnightly* had 'begged Sissy to try to find another'. It is an effective deepening of the irony.

Also inserted in the novel is a gratuitous comment before the vicar replies to Tess's question about the efficacy of her baptism:

Having the natural feelings of a tradesman at finding that a job he should have been called in for had been unskilfully botched by his customers among themselves, he was disposed to say no. (p. 147)

Again we are aware of the bias, the analogy with the tradesman and the ironic use of 'natural' effectively putting down the man subdued by the cloth. But having inserted the sentence above, Hardy adds another in the novel which again has an immediate irony for Tess's situation:

Hearing of the baby's illness, he had conscientiously gone to the house after nightfall to perform the rite, and, unaware that the refusal to admit him had come from Tess's father and not from Tess, he could not allow the plea of necessity for its irregular administration. (p. 147)

Even this addition is perhaps meant to indicate the limitations of Christian practice, Hardy suggesting that going by the book was the negation of genuine feeling. But in the dialogue between Tess and the Vicar which follows in both versions the emotional anguish of the scene is unbearable. From the original Hardy alters 'parochial reasons' to the seemingly weaker 'certain reasons', though this does extend the emphasis to a universal denial of reassurance. More positively Tess's 'saint to sinner' is an impassioned strengthening of the original 'person to sinner', even the alliteration having the impulsive verve which characterizes so many of Tess's utterances. This one is direct and simple, but we are aware of Hardy's overview in the warmly evocative exchange: parsons constrained by rules or dogma are small men, not saints, but this small man rises above the cloth when he gives Tess the comfort her innocent Christian observance requires.

The final paragraph of the chapter shows Hardy looking closely again at his magazine version, and re-shaping and altering in the interests of his main bias. The burial of the baby provides the opportunity for the personalized, omniscient insertion: the bland 'in that shabby corner of the enclosure where the nettles grow' becomes 'in that shabby corner of God's allotment where He lets the nettles grow'. It will be seen from the examination above that Hardy's thematic concerns and his intimate identification with Tess are strengthened by the alterations, and that his own voice comes through unmistakably sure and clear. In *Tess* there is an aesthetic completeness and complexity of relevance, and this concern is seen in Hardy's continuing attentiveness to detail.

In the novel, the precursor of 'The Midnight Baptism', the cause which produces the tragic effect, is 'Saturday Night in Arcady', which was published in the *National Observer*, Special Literary Supplement, of 14 November 1891. It differs markedly from the version in the novel, the opening describing a situation which approximates to Tess's but without narrative decoration. It is assertive, direct précis:

He was masterful, supercilious, coarse; and Big Beauty (as she was called) could not bring herself to encourage him. But he won her. This was how and when.

There follows a description of the farm and the rustic community, similar in first printing and novel, but the additions in the novel are significant and show how consciously Hardy lived in the situation of his heroine in this first crisis. Beauty only goes to Chaseborough once, Tess, after her initial resistance, a few times. Tess responds to her own need for company, which is 'contagious' after her monotonous existence looking after the poultry for the blind Mrs d'Urberville. She is much noticed because of her beauty, but always seeks companionship at nightfall for the return to Trantridge. Hardy's additions here include the significant fact that the Chaseborough market on this Saturday evening in September (month not given in *National Observer*) coincides with a fair, and this gives the tipplers an additional excuse for staying later. As Tess approaches the hay-trusser's she passes Alec d'Urberville on a street corner, and tells him that she is seeking company for her homeward journey. Ironically (in view of the earlier version) he calls her 'my Beauty' and tells her, ominously we may feel, '"I'll see you again"' (p. 106). This is not in the *National Observer*, but thereafter the description of the silent dancing and Beauty's/Tess's question of the Sileni '"when be any of you going home?"' (p. 107) are the same. After the tumble of the dancing couple there are minor variants, and although the watching Alec ('the son of her employer' originally) claims her again as 'my Beauty' in the novel she is only 'mine' earlier. In each instance he is rebuffed, but in the novel his presence is taken note of by the company. This brings them to an awareness of the passage of time.

The descriptions of the group as they move along the road approximate closely in each version. But even here one feels that Hardy displays a self-critical awareness. For instance, the sentence which begins 'They followed the road with a sensation that they were soaring along in a supporting medium . . .' (p. 110) was earlier 'While they marked the road with a pattern like the map of St Paul's course in the Euroclydon . . .' Presumably Hardy cut this as being inappropriate to the narrative atmosphere required in the novel, yet the Biblical nature of the reference is typical of his manner. Car's accident with the treacle is perhaps a little more erotic in the earlier version, where she throws herself down on her back on the grass, 'dragging herself hither and thither upon her elbows, to wipe the hind part of her bodice and gown as well as she could without taking them off'. Car, however, is soon to display her 'faultless rotundities' as prelude to challenging Tess to fight. Tess refuses, 'with dignity' as Beauty, but 'majestically' as Tess, anxious to get away from her 'dear friends' in the first and 'the whole crew' in the second. In the novel we move from Chapter X into Chapter XI with the words 'The twain cantered along for some time without speech' (p. 114), with the earlier version having the girl clinging 'to her knight still panting in her triumph', the irony of 'knight' not being restored or retained by Hardy. But the *National Observer* prints a variant which Hardy must have later discarded. This is before the seduction.

At the rise they met a pedestrian going in the opposite direction; but as he passed behind their backs neither of the two observed him.

When they had withdrawn he turned and looked after them, which he had plenty of time to do . . . He resumed his journey towards the town, and from that moment no living soul saw either of the pair till noon on the day following, when Big Beauty was perceived for a minute or two in the garden by some of her fellow villagers who had walked with her the night previous.

Although discarded in the novel, it is tempting to think of the pedestrian as the man who recognizes Tess on New Year's Eve, later identified as

Farmer Groby. It would have fitted neatly into the pattern of coincidences which characterizes Hardy's tragic manner.

The rest of Chapter XI moves inexorably towards the seduction, with Alec leading Tess into the Chase, his treachery immediately apparent to her, although she is mollified despite herself when he tells her that her father 'has a new cob' (p. 117). It closes with the superb omniscient commentary which acts as cover for the forcing of Tess. In the *National Observer* episode there is none of this, but what there is shows how cleverly Hardy adjusted his intentions. Big Beauty, observed by her fellow field-women, is 'pale and thoughtful', she is now 'even glad of their friendship' and 'She resented nothing that they said to her.' But the close of the episode shows her reduced, abject, dependent, deserted:

> They observed that to him she was deferential thenceforward, that she started when he came into the field, and when he joked jokes of the most excruciating quality she laughed with a childlike belief in them.
>   Two or three months afterwards she was called away from the farm to her native place, many miles off, by the sickness of a relative, which necessitated her engagement there. He made no objection to her going, and on parting she gave him her mouth to kiss, not her cheek, as at one time. She implored him not to desert her. He said he would not; that the parting would not be for long; that he should soon come to see her.
>   But he never went.

Readers will at once recognize the contrast between this and the version in the novel proper; perhaps it reflects Hardy's original intentions, but whether that is so or not Beauty is shadowy, even stereotyped. Hardy's own emotional involvement with his character has clearly not gone beyond a somewhat generalized sympathy for her situation. Beauty is lacking in spirit and has already lost her pride; the word 'deferential' could not in any case be applied to Tess, who would have been unlikely to respond to the jokes, though 'childlike' is a word which we would associate with her. The calling away, even in an episode, is feeble, while Beauty's accepting the kiss on the mouth compares with Tess's only allowing one on the cheek; and in an ironic sense Tess, carrying the secret of her pregnancy with her, deserts Alec rather than vice versa. She tells him that she won't return, a difference indeed from Beauty's imploring her seducer to stay in the *National Observer* piece. The development of the heroine from that sad and diminished prototype is seen in the accretion of spiritedness. Tess turns on Alec in spirited rejection:

'I have said that I will not take anything more from you, and I will not – I cannot! I *should* be your creature to go on doing that, and I won't!' (p. 125)

It is obvious that Hardy developed the skeletal outline of the seduced girl into a fuller, fleshed out emotional study of her situation. What is interesting is the emphasis – the degree of change – from initial unwillingness to complete subjection in the first instance, and from unwillingness to rejection and independent action in the second. It is true that Hardy is making a point in 'Saturday Night in Arcady' which is exemplified throughout the novel, namely that 'the woman pays', the seduced girl being abandoned; this is the way of her world. But in the novel the seduced girl opts for a course of action which reflects a striking individuality and moral courage. She must know – or at least suspect – that she is pregnant; she was forced by Alec on a Saturday night in September, and leaves Trantridge to return home on a Sunday morning in late October. The explicit time-scale may be an indication of Tess's firm morality, an underlining of the 'pure woman' motif. To leave her seducer because she considers it right to do so is a decision which her previous behaviour – and later reactions – would support. It seems likely that Hardy's artistic, emotional and moral identification with his heroine so coalesced that from 'The Maiden' to 'Maiden No More' he gave her those character traits which establish the consistency of her being in the mind of the reader. She is real and ideal. Both 'The Midnight Baptism' and 'Saturday Night' are integral to the novel: they show Hardy having his say, but they also show the early stages of his novel's development. With their adjustments and expansions they become fully integrated into *Tess of the d'Urbervilles*. Read as episodes they particularize; integrated they particularize Tess but universalize by implication, representing emotional, sympathetic and symbolic patterning of a high artistic order. They stress the fact that the woman pays, Hardy's title for 'Phase the Fifth' of the novel. The seduction or rape is the exacting payment of the moment, the baptism and death of Sorrow the consequence. In enumerating the payments thus baldly in the separate pieces, Hardy was signalling the strength of his sympathetic commitment as well as his contempt for the hypocrisy which forced him into such self-censorship. The episodes ironically complement each other in the same way – sequentially – as the phase headings in the novel. And by printing the two crisis points which form the hinges of his plot, Hardy is exposing by innuendo the double standards of man and society. What is clear in the episodes and in *Tess* is that the 'fallen' woman has to find her own means of survival, whether she is rejected or rejects. And the message of 'The Midnight Baptism' is surely that the Anglican Church puts dogma before sincerity. The stigma of illegitimacy remains; Sis, Tess live on, outwardly stained, inwardly scarred. Episodes and novel underline woman as victim of man's sexual indulgence.

The object of concentrating here so closely on what Hardy wrote and then restored or expanded is to make readers aware of his artistic sense on the one hand and the quality of his supportive sympathy on the other. Hardy's explanatory note to the first edition (November 1891) thanks the periodicals which printed the 'episodic sketches' for 'enabling me now to piece the trunk and limbs of the novel together, and print it complete, as originally written two years ago'. In view of his many tinkerings with the text, it matters little whether he is referring to detail or not. What he is referring to, there is no doubt, is the spirit in which his novel was conceived. And it is interesting that the image of 'the trunk and limbs' should be used by him so baldly here. It suggests that mention of the body may not be made in fiction, and the dry humour here is a pathological note on dismembering by convention.

Contemporary Critical Reception

Tess sold excellently but attracted mixed reviews, which reflect convention sometimes failing to come to terms with what Hardy had given them, or enlightened responses which recognized the greatness of the novel despite what were felt to be its blemishes. Richard le Gallienne, writing in the *Star* (23 December 1891), criticized Hardy's style, picking out 'sudden moments of self-consciousness in the midst of his creative flow' and recording also his fondness for scientific and philosophical terminology. Sensitive to the sound and shape of certain words, he stigmatized 'prestidigitation', 'dolorifuge', 'heliolatries' and 'the horrid verb "extasize"'. One is inclined to agree that these are verbal spots on the 'trunk and limbs', but le Gallienne thinks that this is the ' very best' of Hardy's novels, that it has a beautiful simplicity when 'he forgets he is writing', and that although the novel is special pleading for the woman's cause Tess is 'the most satisfying of all Mr Hardy's heroines'. The reviewer in the *Pall Mall Gazette* went further, considering that Angel was not 'altogether a convincing creation, especially when looked at by the side of Tess, whose verisimilitude in art and human quality is maintained throughout with a subtlety and a warm and live and breathing naturalness which one feels to be the work of a tale-teller born and not made'. Here the interest lies in the linking of 'art and human quality'. There is much praise for the rustic chorus and 'the wonderful descriptions of Wessex scenery in the change of the seasons', together with a brave, independent assertion which must have warmed Hardy's heart, in which he deplores the fact that 'the strongest English novel of many years should have to be lopped into pieces ... before it succeeded in finding a complete hearing'. The *Athenaeum* (9 January 1892) thought it 'not only good but great', though 'his use of scientific and ecclesiastical terminology grows excessive'. Reviewing on the same date in the *Illustrated London News*, Clementina Black noted the 'profound moral earnestness' of *Tess*, and after stating that the conventional reader wishes to be excited but not disturbed, that he likes to be presented with pictures rather than new ideas, she goes on to praise the backgrounds and descriptions, and then says:

Yet these, characteristic as they are, are not the essence of the book. Its essence lies in the perception that a woman's moral worth is measured not by any one deed, but by the whole aim and tendency of her life and nature. In regard to men the doctrine is no novelty; the writers who have had eyes to see and courage to declare the same truth about women are rare indeed; and Mr Hardy in this novel has shown himself to be one of that brave and clear-sighted minority.

We should praise the courage of this reviewer for stating so early, and so directly, what has become moral and critical currency from the middle of the twentieth century onwards.

Adverse comments were just as common. The *Saturday Review* (16 January 1892) found that 'there is not one single touch of nature either in John Durbeyfield or in any other character in the book', while Hardy 'tells an unpleasant story in an unpleasant way'. The conception of the 'pure woman' provoked disapproval and moral comment generally, a critic like R. H. Hutton (in *The Spectator*, 23 January 1892) suggesting that Tess could not be truthfully described in this way. But he praised the realism and the descriptions, though he felt that the 'pictures of almost unrivalled power ... evidently proceed from the pantheistic conception that impulse is the law of the universe, and that will, properly so-called, is non-existent fiction'. Andrew Lang's notice in the *New Review* (February 1892) criticizes the style and the content (why should people who are drinking beer be said to 'seek vinous bliss'?) and Mrs Oliphant in *Blackwood's* (March 1892), while praising the 'scent and flavour of the actual', considers Angel a 'pale image', thinks it remarkable that Tess's past was not known at Talbothays, dislikes the ending ('two volumes of analysis and experience are lost, and the end is worse than the beginning'), and finds that 'Mr Hardy's indignant anti-religion becomes occasionally very droll, if not amusing.' Mowbray Morris (see p. 1), as we might expect, takes up the style and finds Angel's 'prestidigitation' remark 'one of the most unconsciously comic sentences ever read in print'. Of Tess he says that 'she never drew breath in any fields trod by human foot', while his overview of Hardy's manner is that he has told 'an extremely disagreeable story in an extremely disagreeable manner'. These shafts are subjective, reflecting an inability to rise above the current imposed limitations, but W. P. Trent's incisive analysis of *Tess* is one of the first to point out Hardy's derivations from classical tragedy. After observing that Tess is 'the greatest character in recent fiction', he says 'it seems as if this modern Englishman was really a Greek endowed with the power of personifying the trees and streams . . . just as he seems to be a Greek in his never-ceasing sense of the presence of an inexorable fate'. This early recognition is reinforced with two more positive evaluations, namely Hardy's 'wonderful power of describing and interpreting inanimate nature' and his realistic delineation of his woman characters.

Andrew Lang was moved to reply to Hardy's preface to the single-volume edition of *Tess*, which was published in September 1892. He dislikes the ending and Hardy's phrase about the 'President of the Immortals', finds the novel distasteful (the word reveals his incapacity) and proceeds to demolish the characterization: 'Poor Tess, a most poetical if not very credible character, is a rural Clarissa Harlowe who wears the parasol and the pretty slippers of iniquity.' In terms of realism, the men are no better: 'The villain Alec and the prig Angel Clare seem to me equally unnatural, incredible, and out of the course of experience.' The style, scientific language and philosophical contemplation, are also put down, while the quality of Alec's dialogue when Tess tells him of the baby attracts justified criticism: 'Ever since you told me of that babe of ours, it is just as if my emotions which have been flowing in a strong stream heavenward, have suddenly found a sluice open in the direction of you through which they have at once gushed.' Hardy's alterations later (see p. 408) are hardly an improvement. Lang's subjectivity, his lack of critical perspective or humanitarian sympathy, are warmly attacked by D. F. Hannigan in the *Westminster Review* (December 1892), though the latter exaggerates himself in rushing to Hardy's defence: 'There is no coarseness in it, no nastiness of detail, and yet nothing essential is avoided . . . We can follow her career as if we knew her and lived with her. We feel her sufferings; we respect her shortcomings; we lament the chain of circumstances that led to her doom; and finally, we forgive and pity her.' If this last is not

quite full enough, much of the rest is spirited, even to the moral condemnation of those who would regard *Tess* as immoral: 'The knowledge
of Nature shown by the author is as wonderful as it is rare' . . . 'the
greatest work of fiction produced in England since George Eliot died',
and, finally, 'Mrs Grundy and her numerous votaries must, for a time
at least, hang their heads in shame.'

The range of contemporary comments anticipates the main directions
of Hardy criticism in the twentieth century, with adverse commentary
diminishing in proportion to the increase in Hardy's reputation and the
evaluation of *Tess* in his *opus*. Although I shall refer to selected modern
criticism in passing, the main emphasis of the following study will be on
Hardy's artistic and human affiliations in his novel, his sense of structure and his sense of life: it is, I believe, the successful integration of
these which make *Tess* one of the great novels of all time.

Tess of the d'Urbervilles

Narrative Structures

1. The Centrality of the Heroine

David Skilton rightly emphasizes (p. 498) that *Tess* did not reach its final form until the Wessex edition of 1912. By that time Hardy had completed his adjustments, more properly called 'tinkerings', and the 'Phases' of Tess's existence, the consistency and overall coherence of her presentation, were established. Since the novel's sequence is chronological, with the retrospect carefully integrated into the graphic action, it seems sensible to look at each Phase as contributing cumulatively to the unfolding fullness of Tess's character, both through the revelations of her consciousness and in her outward social personality. The central focus on the heroine is apparent from the Phase titles, which reflect the main title, generally in an obvious way but in one instance with some subtlety. The first five, from 'The Maiden' to 'The Woman Pays', are each in the obvious category, with 'The Woman Pays' a sounding-board identification with Tess in her immediate and resultant adversity. The emphasis on the word 'maiden' echoes Hardy's inserted subtitle 'A Pure Woman', while 'The Rally' denotes the Talbothays period some two or so years after the death of Sorrow, with Tess soon established in the lush pastures, indulging her love for Angel or reduced to self-accusatory guilt about it. 'The Consequence' embodies the effect of that love and the past concealment, the climax coming at the end of the Phase with Tess's unflinching confession to Angel. The dramatic stroke of having 'The Woman Pays' open with Angel's reception of Tess's story is a telling one: after this the suffering of the pure woman is emotional, psychological and then physical as her means of subsistence are reduced. It is the sixth Phase which carries the heavy irony. 'The Convert' shows the result of Mr Clare's influence on Alec (an influence which he could not exert on his own son), but Alec's sensual nature cannot be converted to a permanent denial of the flesh. The reappearance of Tess reveals at once how fragile is Alec's spiritual will, but the more subtle irony is seen in the fact that Alec's pursuit of her is a rerun of his initial seduction: this had ended in her unwilling 'conversion' to his will, but after resistance she had fled from him. In this sequence she cannot escape: she is reduced by her attenuated existence at Flintcomb-Ash, her abortive pilgrimage to Emminster Vicarage, the news of Angel's invitation to Izz Huett and his continuing and apparently cold silence. But, as in the earlier Phase, there is the economic plight of her family following her father's death. The Phase here ends with Tess and the children on the bedstead by the d'Urberville Aisle. Hardy, in a black inversion of his Phase title, has Tess become a convert to Alec's morality in the name of her family. The descendant of the ancient d'Urbervilles has been superficially converted to the world of the false d'Urberville.

The last Phase, 'Fulfilment', compounds the ironies of the previous one. Tess, in her simple way, is the religious girl forced to embrace sin by the pressures of guilt. The title defines the coming together in temporary happiness (and sexual fulfilment) of Tess and Angel as they wander from her crime. But there is also the submerged sense of fulfilment which Tess experiences from the killing of Alec and the fulfilment exacted by the law, the death of the pure woman in final payment. The Phase titles all focus on Tess, giving her the central presence at all levels of the structure. They are indicators, signposts; obvious, interactive and subtle. They give Tess, and Hardy's conception of her, an indelible consistency.

The term 'phase' therefore encompasses each material, moral and spiritual experience of Tess. The fullness of Hardy's presentation means that present contemplation of his heroine is matched by retrospective emphasis, the first Phase here being important in establishing this duality. This is seen in the opening chapter, where the localized historical circumstances are prelude to Tess's tragedy: the new knowledge debases and subtly prepares us for the coming debasement of Tess, what the conventional moralist would define as the loss of her purity. The family is 'different'; Tess's own difference is sounded factually and symbolically, for she 'wore a red ribbon in her hair, and was the only one of the white company who could boast of such a pronounced adornment' (p. 51). This sets her apart, and the red motif which runs throughout the structure of the novel is early set in motion. She shows in embarrassed reflex her capacity to deceive, telling the lie that '"our own horse has to rest today"' (p. 51) to offset the tipsy spectacle her father presents. And at the same time there is the flash of temper which is later to break out when d'Urberville pesters her and, tragically, when she kills him. The Tess we see in reaction is complemented by the Tess of authorial description, Hardy's emphasis underlining the consistency of conception already indicated. Consider this:

Phases of her childhood lurked in her aspect still. As she walked along today, for all her bouncing handsome womanliness, you could sometimes see her twelfth year in her cheeks, or her ninth sparkling from her eyes; and even her fifth would flit over the corners of her mouth now and then. (p. 52)

Hardy's style in *Tess* is an uneven one, and here there is some labouring for effect, yet given the effect, it is a sure way of underlining Tess's innocence before the experience of Alec. It looks forward to a considered evaluation of her state during the baptism of Sorrow, simply described by Hardy as 'a child's child' (p. 144). The major factor in Tess's girlhood is that the girl appears to be the woman she is not. In aiming at fullness (and subserving his ironic conception) Hardy allows Tess innocence together with a kind of longing for experience: for example, when Angel does *not* dance with her on the green we are told her 'own large orbs wore, to tell the truth, the faintest aspect of reproach that he had not chosen her' (p. 54). The forward-looking irony is characteristic of Hardy's art and presentation of Tess, and it is compounded by the unknown Angel's view of her – 'She was so modest, so expressive' (p. 55). This is to be the foundation of his love for her later, his register of appearance enabling him to idealize the dairymaid at the expense of the woman.

The Durbeyfield domestic context makes Tess a girl-mother before she is forced and becomes one. Sensitive to her father's behaviour, anxious about what may have happened, oppressed by the sordid interior which constitutes their family life, Hardy shows us at once that capacity for guilt which is to dominate her maturity – here the greening of her white frock for which she feels 'a dreadful sting of remorse' (p. 57). With her father's need to get up his strength, and her mother's having to join him, Tess takes on what we assume is a daily responsibility. Her innocence and vulnerability are also stressed, since she senses that her mother's recourse to *The Compleat Fortune-Teller* is prompted by the ancestral revelation, but does 'not divine that it solely concerned herself', a phrase which does not occur in the *Graphic* version. This addition shows Hardy's concern with every stage of Tess's development: it is another stress mark of innocence, of difference, and of limitation. I choose the last word since Tess is sometimes regarded as being too idealized; this addition shows that her lack of awareness, her failure to read others because of the oppressions within herself, brings down upon her *some* of the events which make her tragedy. This is seen again in the description of her imaginative capacity – this complements her modest educational achievements – and underlines the intimacy of Hardy's identification with her:

Tess looked out of the door, and took a mental journey through Marlott. The village was shutting its eyes. Candles and lamps were being put out everywhere: she could inwardly behold the extinguisher and the extended hand. (p. 62)

17

In a sense, this is the first of the journeys undertaken by Tess, a reflective, imaginative inwardness here reaching out before the onset of suffering forces her to look in upon herself. It is one of the most important aspects of her character, soon to be tragically demonstrated by the dozing dream. Before that journey of collision, however, Tess makes her first short journey to Rolliver's, unaware that her 'fine prospects' have already been aired. Disturbed after their return home by her mother's waking her to say that her father can't take the beehives (she is 'lost in a vague interspace between a dream and this information', p. 67), Tess responds immediately and sets out with Abraham. The child's loquacity and his natural reiteration of what he has heard (the idea of Tess marrying a gentleman is repeated five times) calls forth Tess's impatience and her inherent pessimism. The collision with the mailcart and the death of Prince confirm her fatalism: she blames her self-absorption for the accident, and that too contains a prophetic element:

Then, examining the mesh of events in her own life, she seemed to see the vanity of her father's pride; the gentlemanly suitor awaiting herself in her mother's fancy; to see him as a grimacing personage, laughing at her poverty, and her shrouded knightly ancestry. (p. 70)

She is splashed with Prince's blood, full of self-blame, regretting that she has 'danced and laughed only yesterday' (p. 72). Here Hardy is intent on establishing Tess's obsession with guilt, and that she is so 'blighted' by fate, that she cannot get outside herself except through the dangerous reveries which lead her to 'the self-reproach which she continued to heap upon herself for her negligence' (p. 72). The reiteration – 'Nobody blamed Tess as she blamed herself' (p. 73) – firmly fixes the dominant character trait. It is prophetically accentuated at the burial of Prince: 'Her face was dry and pale, as though she regarded herself in the light of a murderess' (p. 73). It is the intensity with which she feels this that shows what she is to feel later; the implication is that she is easily oppressed by the present, and here the emphasis on the economic burden of the family is the major part of her suffering.

Tess is always conscious not only of what she has done but what she thinks she has done. Joan Durbeyfield plays on her daughter's susceptibility, and Tess's guilt makes her respond, despite her pride, to her mother's importunity. Joan's moral blackmail works despite the girl's dislike of being cast as a poor relation. Tess's pride is not of family: it is more of an individual texture, a consciousness of moral right and wrong which seems to be derived from her education, her imagination, elements of religion and the immediate degrading contrast produced by her family. Raymond Williams has rightly pointed out that Tess is not a peasant girl 'seduced by the squire, she is the daughter of a lifeholder and small dealer who is seduced by the son of a retired manufacturer'. He also asserts that the social forces at work in the community condition her fate, while Douglas Brown goes further and says that 'she is the agricultural community in its moment of ruin'. In the initial stages of the novel, the personal *and* the economic pressures are interactive, and later too (at Flintcomb-Ash for instance) we are aware of Hardy's relentless emphasis on the flesh and the spirit.

Hardy uses Tess's first journey to Trantridge to integrate her more fully into her natural inheritance. Brief retrospect shows her 'much loved by others of her own sex and age' (p. 76), but the positive weight is thrown on her working capacity to help support the family. Tess is a girl for all seasons, and it is both natural and fateful that she should go to Trantridge. There, as she contemplates the house and surroundings, Hardy stresses her inexperience, calling her 'simple Tess Durbeyfield' and referring to her 'artlessness' (p. 77). Her dream 'of an aged and dignified face' (p. 79) contrasts with the reality she soon meets in Alec, who quickly exposes her vulnerability and inexperience by his attentions. Tess's reluctant acceptance of the strawberry is another small link in the forecasting chain (p. 81), but again Hardy's subtlety is evident. Tess moves into the kind of mood of will-less acceptance; in other words, she passes beyond resistance, eating in a 'half-pleased, half-reluctant state' (p. 81). Her next reaction is even more significant after Alec plies her with blossoms to put in her bosom:

She obeyed like one in a dream, and when she could affix no more, he himself tucked a bud or two into her hat, and heaped her basket with others in the prodigality of his bounty. (p. 81)

The seeming innocent bounty is a bribing of Tess's senses, Alec propitiating her with gifts of nature (in itself ironic) which leads to the languor, the dream-state which so often seems a refuge from reality for Tess. This acceptance sensuously forecasts the later succumbing: the look forward is deliberate and symbolic, for Tess's languor, dream-state, means that the bastard gift of nature, the brief span of Sorrow the Undesired is thrust upon her. Innocence becomes experience. And Hardy's sense of the grotesque interconnectedness of situation is shown in the fact that when Tess gets into the van she presents a spectacle to her fellow passengers, a contrast she is later to present to the villagers of Marlott when she has her baby. This detailed tracing of connection is seen too in the comment that 'she rode along with an inward and not an outward eye' (p. 84). Her dream-like state even here is a refuge from reality. But she cannot escape it; she becomes aware of what she looks like, and then 'in looking downwards a thorn of the rose remaining in her breast accidentally pricked her chin ... Tess was steeped in fancies and prefigurative superstitions; she thought this an ill omen – the first she had noticed that day' (p. 84). This simple shedding of blood is obviously prefigurative in the structural symbolism – Hardy believes artistically in using what his heroine believes naturally – here linked to the loss of virginity, the compassionate killing of the birds, the murder of Alec. It is a further underlining of the aesthetic and sophisticated nature of Hardy's art *and* the warmth of his imaginative identification with Tess. The artistic medium is made to reflect the rustic mind; superstitions, like novels, are vigorous with life. There are a number of instances in the novel where Tess's reactions and words are Hardy's feelings and thoughts not *of* her situation but *in* it: the revelations are from within. She is a successful and compelling character almost against the odds of her conception, for she is at once real, ideal and symbolic. Hardy's genius ensures that there is no dislocation or disintegration for the reader. His presentation of her is such that we accept the multiplicity of the conception without querying the components.

The sense of foreboding which is present in much of the novel is particularized in Tess. There is a natural poignancy about her simply expressed fears – '"I would rather stay here with father and you"' (p. 86) – while her walking in the garden among the gooseberry bushes and over Prince's grave exemplifies her obsessive guilt. In a sense she blackmails herself; we feel that she gets some pleasure in the penance that involves risk. When she decides to go to Trantridge she comes out of her abstraction but refuses to take her mother's hopes for her future seriously. Again the consistency in detail – structural comprehensiveness – is present. When she prepares for her second fateful journey to Trantridge her mother is delighted to wash her hair and to make the most of her. Tess's response – '"Do what you like with me, mother"' (p. 89) – is an unconscious acceptance of the fuller burden she is later to bear. The continuing notation of Tess's immaturity is seen when the frock Joan puts on her 'imparted to her developing figure an amplitude which belied her age, and might cause her to be estimated as a woman when she was not much more than a child' (p. 89). The child/woman who is mother to her mother's children is also dreamer/practical worker in the family situation which is always at the back of her wherever she goes. But she is warm with this family affection and full of regret (and not just foreboding) at leaving them; she is an emotional and loving girl (her mother considers her 'such an odd maid', p. 90) with the individual pride already noted. Her sensitivity is shown again when we feel her distaste at her father's offers to sell his title, made grotesque by his diminishing demands. She is insecure and upset, saying goodbye to her father 'with a lumpy throat' (p. 90), while after his offers we are told that her 'eyes were too full and her voice too choked to utter the sentiments that were in her. She turned quickly, and went out' (p. 91). It is interesting to note that the words 'bitter reproaches' were in the *Graphic* for the 'sentiments' of the revision. Once more we see Hardy working on Tess in his revision, since 'sentiments' is a softening from 'bitter reproaches', which would have given a twist to her character. It would have made her less warm, impulsive (which she is), but capable of nursing a grievance, which she is not. Hardy's revision is largely employed in giving Tess consistency.

Before she gets in the gig under Alec's persuasion, the foreboding (called here 'misgiving') returns to complicate her reactions. Then, in the full power of her obsessive guilt, 'Something seemed to quicken her to a determination: possibly the thought that she had killed Prince. She suddenly stepped up; he mounted beside her, and immediately whipped on the horse' (p. 92). What follows shows the power of Tess's resistant pride and Hardy's careful structural building, always with the edge of prophecy in mind. The whipping of the mare rouses Tess's spirit (in a sense she is Tib, used and beaten), but Alec's explanation why he has such a horse is also part of the structural coherence:

'It was my fate, I suppose. Tib has killed one chap; and just after I bought her she nearly killed me. And then, take my word for it, I nearly killed her.' (p. 95)

This story within the story touches Tess here and in the future: it is an oblique summary, with differences, of the novel we are reading. But here Alec's immediacy and his pressures on Tess to yield are all prefigurative. Her eyes are 'like those of a wild animal', she yields to 'the kiss of mastery' (p. 96), precursor of more serious forcing, and she wipes the spot where he has kissed her. Hardy's comment is 'She had, in fact, undone the kiss, as far as such a thing was physically possible' (p. 97). This underlines another consistent characteristic, Tess's attempts to 'undo' what has passed, seen patently in the move to Talbothays where she can work away from her past. It prefigures her confession to Angel on her wedding evening, but here she is hemmed in by Alec's gig, and can only cry out with spirit: '"I don't like 'ee at all! I hate and detest you! I'll go back to mother, I will!"' (p. 98). Even the mixed register, the "ee" and 'you' show the frantic divisions and fear within Tess. These are the words of a child for whom there is no going back, no return from the perilous journey to womanhood.

Tess's misgivings are accentuated when she realizes that Alec's mother is blind, but even here her imaginative capacity is used. When she gives the old lady the birds we are told:

It reminded Tess of a Confirmation, in which Mrs d'Urberville was the bishop, the fowls the young people presented, and herself and the maid-servant the parson and curate of the parish bringing them up. (p. 101)

It may be that her own confirmation is in her mind, but the ritual, the form her imagination takes, is interesting in revealing her need to be associated with the few simple ceremonies that she knows. It prepares us for her intensity over the baptism of Sorrow. The imaginative flair shown here, like her dreams, self-absorptions, obsessions, is part of her sensitivity and superstition, with the religious practice of her childhood a natural conditioning of her mind. Tess looking after the birds learns a language of communication, the whistling bringing her close to their natures; but this practice of innocence with the live birds is the precursor of experience with the dying birds. Then Tess learns another language, the silent strangling of death. For Hardy, as for her, the reflex communication signals the capacity for compassion which ennobles Tess.

The Chaseborough sequence (Chapters X and XI) has already been discussed (see pp. 5–9) but there are a few additional comments relevant here. It is important to note that Tess's life at Trantridge is largely a solitary one, though she finds outlets in companionship and enjoyment. Her sexual attractions are stressed, an underlining of her vulnerability, something of which she is aware, for 'she always searched for her fellows at nightfall, to have the protection of their companionship homeward' (p. 105). Fate provides the coincidence of market and fair, and fate provides Tess with spontaneous and ill-considered amusement at the spectacle of Car Darch trying to get the treacle off her gown. Here Hardy uses a dated convention when he writes 'Our heroine, who had hitherto held her peace, at this wild moment could not help joining in with the rest' (p. 111). The clichéd, mannered tone is perhaps employed to emphasize Tess's own moral and spiritual distance from this company, which she is quick to utter ('"and if I had known you was of that sort, I wouldn't have so let myself down as to come with such a whorage as this is!"' p. 112). As a contemporary critic remarked, Tess's choice of the word 'whorage' proclaims her sexual earthiness: she is not all innocence, nor could she be, given her domestic and social context. But the use here carries the authorial irony of her immediate fate. Once Alec's 'rescue' of her is accomplished, Tess feels 'inexpressibly weary' (p. 115), and this lassitude is an encouragement to Alec, who supports her by putting his arm round her waist after that 'moment of oblivion' when 'her head sank gently against him' (p. 115). Tess is as impetuous and divided as ever; first she gives him a push, then begs his pardon. She trusts him despite recognizing his treachery, and is further undermined by his '"your father has a new cob to-day"' (p. 117). She feels gratitude and repugnance, falls asleep and is seduced/raped. Hardy's reticence is a mark of outward conformity, but it is also a brilliant universalizing of Tess: the one woman typifies the many who are compelled to suffer the same form of degradation at the hands of man. The tone is bitter, rhetorical, fatalistic, informed with omniscient irony, prefigurative and socially analytic. The end of the first Phase registers the inevitability of Tess's fate, although there are six stages of pure woman to be played out before the final drop.

Tess's return to Marlott draws forth from Hardy the explicit analogy with *The Rape of Lucrece* (p. 123). First there is her listlessness, Hardy's commentary that she no longer fears Alec, and her depression. The death-wish occurs explicitly for the first time ('"I wish I had never been born"', p. 124), and she shows a will to punish herself. She will not be bought, but we observe that she is near confession – '"If I did love you I may have the best o' causes for letting you know it. But I don't"' (p. 126). This hint of pregnancy (apparently unregistered by Alec) also shows her pride, a kind of integrity, a moral difference from her class and situation.

Tess's meeting with the painter of texts – the integration of fate and symbol by Hardy – shows her capacity to indulge her sense of sinfulness. The 'staring vermilion words' (p. 128) have the personal accusatory force which sets off her inward hysteria. She is hypersensitive, ridden by her conscience. There follows the meeting with her disappointed mother. And at this point in the *Graphic* Hardy has Tess describe the mock-marriage she went through with Alec:

'I drove with him to Melchester, and there in a private room I went through the form of marriage with him as before a registrar. A few weeks after, I found out that it was not the registrar's house we had gone to, as I had supposed, but the house of a friend of his who had played the part of the registrar.' (p. 503)

The feebleness of this, and the diminishing of Tess – not just naïveté, but a kind of unthinking stupidity – supports the 'pure woman' motif, for it presupposes cohabitation. But the revision (or restoration) is much more convincing in its striking assertion of Tess's moral independence, her 'purity' of motive. It doesn't stop her upbraiding the feckless Joan with '"I was a child when I left this house four months ago. Why didn't you tell me there was danger in men-folk?"' (p. 131). Hardy supplements her ordeal with descriptive commentary which has been overlooked by some critics:

On matrimony he had never once said a word. And what if he had? . . . She had never wholly cared for him, she did not at all care for him now. She had dreaded him, winced before him, succumbed to adroit advantages he took of her helplessness; then, temporarily blinded by his ardent manners, had been stirred to confused surrender awhile: had suddenly despised and disliked him, and had run away. That was all. (p. 130)

This is admirable in direct clarity, but it omits those conditioning factors which are present in Tess's character throughout. The first of these is the undermining which makes her feel that she *must* repay her parents for the loss of Prince. The 'cob' and the toys for the children are among the 'adroit advantages'. The second factor is the recognition, or part-recognition at least, that she is the plaything of fate and that she is doomed to accept the victim's role in life. This second point is more fully developed in the later stages of the novel, Hardy's ironic master-stroke being that she is only freed from her sense of it by the murder of Alec. His blood-letting brings her a kind of fulfilment, the Phase title capturing it in her brief consummation with Angel and the ultimate fulfilment of death. The summary of Tess's consciousness given above perhaps reflects her self-confusion, and hence somewhat glib explanation, of what she has done.

Tess's inwardness after her return home is finely described, the irony playing over her ephemeral 'triumph' in the eyes of her friends. The description of her response to music and her attendance at church stress the comfort of her imagination and the outward observance cushioning what is to come. Her closeness to nature, the darkness leaving her 'absolute mental liberty' (p. 134) are registers of pathos. But exceptional as she is, there is a suspicion that in his warmth of identification with her Hardy has her express views which are his own or at least with which he has a sympathetic affinity:

She had no fear of the shadows; her sole idea seemed to be to shun mankind – or rather that cold accretion called the world which, so terrible in the mass, is so unformidable, even pitiable, in its units. (p. 134)

She has her individual psychology and a mystical intensity, for 'At times her whimsical fancy would intensify natural processes around her till they seemed a part of her own story. Rather they became a part of it; for the world is only a psychological phenomenon, and what they seemed they were' (p. 134). This is Hardy's thought become Tess's. Her moral awareness, her ever-present sense of wrongdoing, is richly personified in the ambience of nature:

Walking among the sleeping birds in the hedges, watching the skipping rabbits on a moonlit warren, or standing under a pheasant-laden bough, she looked upon herself as a figure of Guilt intruding into the haunts of Innocence. (p. 135)

This identification shows Tess in the grip of her obsessive self-indictment. Hardy's own gloss says that 'She had been made to break an accepted social law' (p. 135) but *not* a law known to nature. Before she moves into the practicality of work, birth (and death) Hardy demonstrates her affinity with nature. It is the most profoundly sympathetic stress in her character.

Tess is sensitively aware in interaction with her companion field-workers. The baby symbolizes her guilt to herself. The divisions, uncertainties and paradoxes within her are probed as she handles the child and contemplates

the far distance ... with a gloomy indifference that was almost dislike: then all of a sudden she fell to violently kissing it some dozens of times, as if she would never leave off, the child crying at the vehemence of an onset which strangely combined passionateness and contempt. (p. 140)

Postnatal depression may be contributory here, but the contradictions are pure Tess. Taken too young for motherhood, and with an omnipresent sense of her sin, Tess's feelings, which often run to the impetuous, here take their natural course: she rarely achieves anything approaching tranquillity, and even the later ecstasies at Talbothays are marred by extremes of depression and apprehension.

Hardy is at pains to underline Tess's lack of perspective, her belief that the 'world' would condemn being 'founded on an illusion' (p. 141). But so is her determination to believe that the past was past, for even in such moments of transient optimism Tess's death-wish is apparent. She sees herself in the future as 'grassed down and forgotten' (p. 141), although for the time being she enjoys the village notoriety of her state. It is in the baptism scene that Tess is most consciously presented by Hardy, her resilience, simple faith, sympathetic actions all unbearably moving despite the idealized nature of the description. She is, as often, at the same time the suffering girl-mother and the symbol of all such.

25

Hardy's use of the word 'immaculate' (p. 145) echoes both the immaculate conception and the subtitle of the novel. The pathos is sublime; to her brothers and sisters she is 'a divine personage with whom they had nothing in common' (p. 146). But this effect is balanced by the 'blemishes which sunlight might have revealed' (p. 144) and afterwards by Tess's impetuous reaction against the clergyman. The sequence is a strong demonstration of Hardy's inability to combine the real and the ideal successfully in his presentation.

A short chapter concludes Phase the Second. It is a curiously heavy-handed chapter, perhaps consonant with Tess's extreme depression in reaction. The death-wish is prominent, the date of her death absorbing her, and underlining her morbid temperament. The past cannot be put down, but she realizes that she must get away to where that past is not known. And here the authorial irony suggests the operation of fate, since Talbothays 'stood not remotely from some of the former estates of the d'Urbervilles . . . All the while she wondered if any strange good thing might come to her being in her ancestral land' (p. 151). This shows her inadvertently embracing her fate, and shows too what is perhaps a seasonal quality of optimism, her resilience. Her youth here is responding to the challenge of life in the present as a means of shutting out the past.

'The Rally' after the 'silent reconstructive years' (p. 155) is in a sense illusory. Although there is much happiness, the submerged past is never forgotten. The moral conscience which motivates her to leave home so that she will not be a corruptive influence on the children ensures that she will continue to think of herself as a sinner. While the inward examination continues, there is an outward corollary to it: Tess rejects another past, that of 'her useless ancestors' (p. 156) when she says of her mother, 'All my prettiness comes from her, and she was only a dairymaid' (p. 156). Both pasts are influential, tragically influential, in her life.

Hardy's description of the Talbothays landscape, its seasonal lushness and its spatial perspective, has its sympathetic affinity with Tess. Her first views of the area increase her well-being, and this journey is seen as a 'pilgrimage' (p. 158). But although the outside is expansive, Tess settling into the dairy finds that reminders of the past are a constant in this present. The Jack Dollop story involving the girl he has wronged disconcerts her as a wronged girl; she is ever-sensitive to such identifications, though we remember that the ballads of her field companions did not distress her. Here the sensitivity is in case someone should find out, whereas there they already knew. But Tess is a developing character, and she shows remarkable intuitive perception in seeing Angel as 'educated, reserved, subtle, sad, differing' (p. 166). As Hardy integrates Angel into the novel, so we notice a fullness of nature in Tess which complements her physical appeal. As well as her 'fluty voice', Angel registers her mystical/superstitious predilections: '"I do know that our souls can be made to go outside our bodies when we are alive"' (p. 175). He sees her though as 'a fresh and virginal daughter of Nature' (p. 176). The irony of this is apparent; the conception, further idealized by Angel as he comes to know Tess better, stresses the appearance as distinct from what he later feels is the dissonant reality. In the *Graphic*, 'genuine' stood for 'fresh and virginal'; there is as so often ironic method in Hardy's 'tinkering'.

With Angel's proximity Tess shows her capacity – occasionally – to enter into an exalted mood. The symbolic garden scene (pp. 178–9) finds her in absorption or reverie again:

Tess was conscious of neither time nor space. The exaltation which she had described as being producible at will by gazing at a star, came now without any determination of hers; she undulated upon the thin notes of the second-hand harp, and their harmonies passed like breezes through her, bringing tears into her eyes. (p. 179)

It is an extended irony that as Clare comes to love her he proposes to take her reading in hand, to make her a cultivated farmer's wife with an engrafted culture of his determining. But Tess is creative in feeling, remarkable in imagination, not enslaved by the doubtful sophistications of the written word. In the early stages of her feelings for Angel she is often morbid and apprehensive, insecure from her past, but vibrant in her fancies: '"The trees have inquisitive eyes, haven't they"' is linked to her fear of the many tomorrows which appear to be saying '"I'm coming! Beware of me! Beware of me!"' (p. 180). The pathos of this prefiguring is evident, an inward sense of Fate which complements the outward circumstances of its inexorable movement. Although Hardy comments in passing that Tess's 'corporeal blight had been her mental harvest' (p. 180) we note that she reaps suffering and a greatly increased susceptibility. She exerts her will ('Tess was trying to lead a repressed life, but she little divined the strength of her own vitality', p. 181). Her conversations with Angel show that bitterness lurks beneath the surface as she questions '"why the sun do shine on the just and the unjust alike"' (p. 182). The ancestral other past haunts her, with Dairyman Crick's unthinking interpretation of Clare's attitude towards old families adding to her insecurity. Despite this we are told that Tess 'had never in her recent life been so happy as she was now, possibly never would be so happy again' and that she and Clare were 'ever balanced on the edge of a passion' (p. 185). The second Jack Dollop story hits her more severely than the first, and she endures solitary agony because of her identification. It calls up her own case, and Tess is given to subjective brooding, trapped by the fear of revelation and shame.

Her oppression makes us increasingly aware that she has never known a light side of life, that where there might have been gaiety and humour there is only the morbid tendency to recur to the past. She is 'deeper-passioned' (p. 194) than the three girls who love him, but is so beset by conscience that she feels that she can never let any man marry her. Tess as victim now embarks on a course of self-sacrifice, drawing Angel's attention to the other girls. At the same time she responds to his scrupulosity and her respect for him increases. But Tess responds to proximity. Angel's carrying of the girls through the flood shows Tess bravely attempting to be independent despite her feelings. She offers to climb along the bank, but she is physically and emotionally susceptible, obviously moved by his ' "Three Leahs to get one Rachel" ' though she replies, with great fortitude, ' "They are better women than I" ' (p. 202). Tess's generosity of spirit is more than skin-deep. In the midst of her own suffering she finds the will to give – 'And yet that same hungry heart of hers compassionated her friends' (p. 204). The verb 'compassionated' defines Tess's capacity (seen later when she kills the birds); it is her warmth and sympathy, so often stifled in the present because of the obtrusion of the past.

Reverie, whether brooding or perhaps vacant, is part of her nature; the outward tranquillity of milking sometimes finds her lost in thought. Hardy indicates her sexual awakening on one of those rare occasions when Angel is impassioned enough to take her in his arms. She responds naturally and uninhibitedly as 'she sank upon him in her momentary joy, with something very like an ecstatic cry' (p. 209). Soon, however, the 'Consequence' is felt, for 'She seemed stilled, almost alarmed, at what had occurred' (p. 213). Although there is a narrative switch to Angel, Tess is never far from our thoughts – or his. He explains and defines Tess to Mr Clare; the tone strikes the present-day reader as a curious mixture of condescension and insight. This is how Angel sees the woman he loves:

'She'll be apt pupil enough, as you would say if you knew her. She's brim full of poetry – actualized poetry, if I may use the expression. She *lives* what paper poets only write . . .' (p. 225)

Tess thus idealized is not complete Tess, as Clare is to discover; she is the woman he *wants* to think she is. Much of the *real* Tess's thoughts and feelings are unknown to him: the medium of her behaviour effectively conceals the message. When he comes back, 'The brimfulness of her nature breathed from her' (p. 231). The sensual images conveying Tess's vital sexuality are ironically mixed by Hardy. She 'was warm as a sunned cat' (p. 232) is superbly direct and felt, but 'while she regarded him as Eve at her second waking might have regarded Adam' (p. 232) is loaded with associations of temptation and deception which take the bloom off febrile innocence.

When she receives Angel's proposal, Tess is disconcerted enough to invoke social subterfuge with her '"your mother wouldn't like you to marry such as me. She will want you to marry a lady"' (p. 233). Tess cannot escape this way, and she feels further trapped when Clare's reference to his father's encounter with a wild young man at '"a place forty miles from here"' who has '"a mother afflicted with blindness"' (p. 235) unconsciously stirs up her past. Here she looks worn, 'her ripe mouth tragical' (p. 235). She wishes someone else would enlighten Clare, yet she adopts his accents and attitudes outwardly and a greater self-suppression too. She experiences 'positive pleasure and positive pain' (p. 239) and she is 'a sheaf of susceptibilities' (p. 239). These susceptibilities and Clare's pressures on her to marry him reduce Tess. This is how Hardy puts it, after she has thrown herself down 'in palpitating misery broken by momentary shoots of joy':

Every see-saw of her breath, every wave of her blood, every pulse singing in her ears, was a voice that joined with nature in revolt against her scrupulousness . . . to snatch ripe pleasure before the iron teeth of pain could have time to shut upon her. (p. 241)

The torture image conveys the agony and the ecstasy. In her consciousness is the intuitive foreknowledge of what may be the 'consequence'. Tess is her own prophet of doom, feeling that she must possess Angel but '"it is a wrong to him, and may kill him when he knows"' (p. 242).

Tess also suffers from the reflex fateful pressures within the dairy at this time. After the next tale about that local legend Jack Dollop Mrs Crick observes, '"Well, the silly body should have told en sooner that the ghost of her first man would trouble him"' (p. 243). The words exactly fit the dilemma of the listening 'sheaf of susceptibilities', who next hears Marian say, '"She ought to ha' told him just before they went to church, when he could hardly have backed out"' (p. 244). Tess's resolve to refuse Angel is temporarily strengthened, but the story helps to set up in Tess 'a religious sense of a certain moral validity in the previous union' (p. 245). This sense is prefigurative of her return to Alec later. She has another sense which makes her see herself as subordinate to Angel, wanting his 'tutelary guidance' and believing (ironic this) that he was 'one who would love and cherish and defend her under any conditions, changes, charges, or revelations' (p. 246). This is Tess's pathetic delusion: Angel is not ready for a love which breaks the ideal image of his making. Tess is not always subdued; when Clare, as part of his 'tutelary guidance' tells her to call him 'Angel dearest' she responds with 'a roguish curl coming upon her mouth, notwithstanding her suspense' (p. 247). It is a delicious hint of a comic spirit, a little bit of innocent devil in the suppressed personality of Tess. The might-have-been, so much a part of Hardy's presentation of character and situation, carries the infinite pathos of deprivation in Tess.

I have mentioned the importance of journeys in the presentation of Tess, and the next fateful one is when Angel agrees to take the milk to the station. This is the day of decision, with Angel's physical closeness and his protecting her against the rain having the immediacy of persuasion. But there is also the fateful mention of the one-time d'Urberville seat to which Clare draws attention. And at this point Hardy encompasses Tess with authorial perspective:

... this unsophisticated girl, with the round bare arms, the rainy face and hair, the suspended attitude of a friendly leopard at pause, the print gown of no date or fashion, and the cotton bonnet drooping on her brow. (p. 251)

This is an impressionistic moment as the engine lights flash on her, the 'leopard' image perfectly conveying her latent sexuality, abused in the past and febrile with suppression in the present. Her determination to lift the suppression and confess is thwarted when Angel's flippant tone about the d'Urberville confession effectively aborts the Durbeyfield one. It is as if the index finger of fate is upon her, aided by her fear, her self-victimization and recognition. The succinct irony which accompanies Angel seizing upon her family connection, which she had expected him to despise, is admirable:

She had not told. At the last moment her courage had failed her, she feared his blame for not telling him sooner; and her instinct of self-preservation was stronger than her candour. (p. 253)

There are many moving moments in the novel, almost all deriving from Tess and her suffering, but I suggest that there is none more directly poignant than her reaction after she has at last agreed to be his wife. It is shot through with anguish, and shows just how 'deeply-passioned' and conscience-stricken she is made by her momentous decision:

She had no sooner said it than she burst into a dry hard sobbing so violent that it seemed to rend her. Tess was not a hysterical girl by any means, and he was surprised. (p. 254)

The irony which follows is almost unbearable. Tess expresses again her agony – '"I sometimes wish that I had never been born!"' – while Clare tells her that she is 'very inexperienced' (p. 255). He compounds this unwittingly when Tess says that she must write to her mother by agreeing and saying, '"You are a child to me, Tess"' (p. 255), ignorant of Joan's lack of moral principle. That lack is shown in her reply to Tess, '"that on no account do you say a word of your Bygone Trouble to him"', to which Tess can only murmur, '"O mother, mother!"' (p. 256). Tess is fated but she is also, despite having a family and a lover, alone. Although she recognizes her mother's spurious advice for what it is, she keeps quiet about her past, indulges the ecstatic moments of the present, believing absolutely in the image she takes for reality in Clare. Hardy's simple commentary here is 'Her affection for him was now the breath and life of Tess's being' (p. 260). But his reassurances are calculated to rekindle Tess's smouldering feelings of guilt, particularly when he says that she is '"numbered among those who are true, and honest, and just, and pure, and lovely, and of good report – as you are, my Tess"' (p. 260). Hardy may be overdoing the irony somewhat here, but the effects on Tess are perhaps exacerbated by the Biblical connotation which she would recognize.

Her generosity of spirit is often shown in her treatment of the other milkmaids, and theirs in response – they cannot hate her because she is chosen by Angel – calls forth bitter tears on her pillow as she resolves once more to tell Angel the truth. But delay is everything, and the accumulations of fate, each one adding to her tremulousness and suffering, each one unseen and unapprehended by Clare, combine to forestall her good intentions. On one occasion Tess and Clare stand on a gravel cliff and hear what appears to be the noises of the populace of a great city below them. Tess explores this fancy: Clare, absorbed 'was not particularly heeding' (p. 267). It is a revealing moment, showing that Clare has no particular thought for what is going on in Tess's mind, this small instance reflecting a deeper ignorance. Tess continues to worship – she catches Angel's 'manner and habits, his speech and phrases, his likings and his aversions' (p. 270). Angel keeps up his pressures on her, deciding that a farmhouse, once a d'Urberville mansion, will serve for their honeymoon: he does not confide in her beforehand about getting a licence instead of having the banns called, but Tess reacts with relief that everything is being set in motion. The morbid apprehension still surfaces though, and she feels that '"All this good fortune may be scourged out of me afterwards by a lot of ill"' (p. 271). When she tries on the gown that Angel has bought her, the words of the ballad about the wife 'That once had done amiss' come into her mind. Tess is her own worst enemy. Her capacity for imaginative recall and fearful or superstitious associations ensures that she is always vulnerable, rarely free from inward suffering.

Two events before the wedding maintain this vulnerability at a high pitch. The first occurs on Christmas Eve when the man from Trantridge (who we meet again later as Farmer Groby – fate operates at all levels) recognizes her and insults her. The incident sets off Angel's dream, and motivates Tess to write him the letter of confession which fatefully goes under the carpet. Again Hardy seems to be pushing too hard, but the effect on Tess of seeing Angel apparently undisturbed is an ironic masterstroke. It maintains the tension, prepares us for the confession having to be made despite the fact that when Tess retrieves the letter she cannot face the immediate reality – 'She could not let him read it now, the house being in full bustle of preparation; and descending to her own room she destroyed the letter there' (p. 277). The action reveals the deep divisions within her. She longs to retain Clare but believes that she has no right to him: the swinging of the moral pendulum makes her volatile, self-sacrificing, silent. Hardy's presentation of her through vacillations, delays and febrile excitement and suffering shows his identification with her moods. She affects a 'lightness' of manner when she tells Angel that she wants to '"confess all my faults and blunders!"' (p. 277). Sadly, ironically, their lack of full concord adds to the tragedy, with the might-have-been element markedly present too. Tess's death-wish has always been the companion of what she regards as her undeserved happiness, illusory, passing, guilt-obfuscated. The immediacy of the wedding is seen through Tess's eyes, the 'boy' of sixty with the running sore on his leg standing as yet another melancholy symbol of fate.

The wedding is focused almost exclusively on Tess's responses and their 'ecstatic solemnity' (p. 279). She moves herself towards Angel as the shadow of fear obtrudes itself upon her. It is at this point that Hardy asserts, outside consciousness but with a reinforcing and definitive omniscience, Angel's ignorance of the 'full depth of her devotion, its single-mindedness, its meekness; what long-suffering it guaranteed, what honesty, what endurance, what good faith' (p. 279).

The words by direct implication cast doubt on whether Clare possesses these qualities or the character to acquire them: this is the obverse side of Tess's tragedy. Irradiated by the bells, Tess soon has to endure Clare's unwitting insensitivity in telling her of the old coach and the d'Urberville legend. Her questioning of him shows apprehension and guilt – '"Is it when we are going to die, Angel, that members of my family see it, or is it when we have committed a crime?"' (p. 280). The unconscious and subconscious prefigurative nature of this shows Hardy's concern for structural detail, yet it is completely in the context of Tess's character and mood. The death–crime obsession has been and is hers: she is going to die to Angel for confessing her crime, and later to die for killing Alec. Alone, without a 'counsellor' (p. 281), Hardy's word, she prays to her God, who is Angel. Her creator, with sure tautness of structure, has her utter words to herself which are to be echoed later by the shattered and sunken Angel – '"for she you love is not my real self, but one in my image; the one I might have been!"' (p. 281). Tess broods on purity with the fixed self-indictment of one who is incapable of seeing outside a supposedly ruined self. We are reminded of the epigraph from *Two Gentlemen of Verona* which Hardy chose for the title-page of *Tess*:

> 'Poor wounded name! My bosom as a bed
> Shall lodge thee.' (I, ii, 115/6)

Julia's tender and loving words here express the constancy and unselfish devotion in love which eventually wins the betraying Proteus back to her. The parallels with Angel and Tess are worth noting, though they need not be unnecessarily delved; Shakespeare brings the lovers together suddenly and Proteus recognizes Julia's worth as Angel – 'too late beloved' – comes to recognize Tess's, both men acknowledging their wrong. But Tess's vibrant sensitivity, her isolation, Angel's inability to respond to her with warmth and generosity of feeling, plus Tess's wilful and willing assumption of the role of victim, all these contribute to the onset of her tragedy. Outside fate contributes too: as she leaves for her aborted honeymoon with Angel, Tess generously asks Angel to kiss her three companions, not realizing what the effect will be. This is followed by the 'afternoon crow' (p. 282) which portends evil and further undermines Tess.

She is always sensitive to atmosphere, and 'the mouldy old habitation' (p. 283) and the portraits with their likenesses and silent record of past offences can hardly lift her mood. Angel can, and the delightful intimacy of their hands mixing in the basin keeps in abeyance her natural

33

morbidity. Hardy's attention to detail here enhances the terrible reversal to come: he altered the 'restless and depressed' description of Tess in the *Graphic* to the more typical 'absent-minded' (p. 285), emphasizing the continuity we have noted earlier – Tess's withdrawal into reverie when she is depressed or excited. The arrival of the jewels on their wedding eve makes her feel that all is well, particularly as Angel shows her how 'to tuck in the upper edge of her bodice' (p. 287), which produces exhilaration and perhaps a greater sexual awareness of herself. The news of the other milkmaids moves her towards confession, for she feels that they 'had deserved better at the hands of Fate. She had deserved worse – yet she was the chosen one' (p. 290). Tess embraces confession but Angel gets there before her, the room a silent register of symbols as she feels, with that imaginative immediacy which is one of her strongest traits that 'He seemed to be her double' (p. 291). Tess, animated, excited, reassured, presses Angel's hand as he tells her his little story; buoyant with hope, she believes that what she has to tell '"cannot be more serious, certainly"' (p. 292). Hardy, alert to his heroine's every pulse-beat, added after this a phrase which was not in the *Graphic*, the truthful, trusting, honest, 'because 'tis just the same!' (p. 292). Her relief is delusory: the woman pays for her sexual transgression, but the man doesn't.

The next Phase heading reflects the immediate and far-reaching extent of Tess's payment. Her direct reaction to Angel's strangled tones and unapproximate language is to ask forgiveness, her simple request echoing the Lord's Prayer, which marked her simple early faith. Clare exacerbates their mutual position by the use of a word outside Tess's register – 'prestidigitation' – and alien to her nature, which is devoid of any form of artifice, followed by the laugh that is like death to her. Her own nobility and selflessness rise above it: the inequality of feeling between them is seen in her impassioned '"having begun to love you, I love you for ever – in all changes, in all disgraces, because you are yourself. I ask no more"' (pp. 298–9). The emotional effort is almost too much for her physically: she cries for herself, but she is also crying for her lost love who, moved to compassion by her tears, is distant now in his own self-pity and pride. Tess is abject in self-denial and prostration, her guilt making her say that she will not follow Angel if he leaves her, but when he does move she follows him impetuously. She feels the touch of the jewels 'as sarcasm', and Hardy now stresses the pathos of her situation by using one of the animal images we associate with her by referring to her 'dumb and vacant fidelity' to Clare (p. 301). Yet when she does come up with Clare she speaks with truthful clarity – her reasoning incisive, a contrast with his – '"I have not told of anything that interferes with or belies my love for you"' (pp. 301–2). She reiterates that she was a child at the time (remember Hardy's emphasis on this), and asserts her natural dignity: '"I am only a peasant by position, not by nature!"' (p. 302). Her threat to commit suicide by drowning shows the re-emergence, hardly surprising, of the death-wish.

The irony of Hardy's presentation now deepens. Tess returns to the house in obedience to Angel's wish and, in her emotionally and physically exhausted state, falls asleep. The irony embraces the might-have-been had she stayed awake. Even asleep she is fated, since Angel has only to look at the tucked-in bodice on one of the portraits of Tess's ancestors to make an immediate moral connection with Tess. The next morning, though distant, he is amazed to see that 'She looked absolutely pure. Nature, in her fantastic trickery, had set such a seal of maidenhood upon Tess's countenance that he gazed with a stupefied air' (p. 307). This superb focus is further evidence of Hardy's attention to detail. We note 'pure' and the adverbial expansion of it, the simple echo of the title-page *after* the confession and Angel's reaction. Interesting also is the fact that Hardy changed the 'girlishness' of the *Graphic* to 'maidenhood' for the book publication, another underlining of his forthright conception. Tess's innocence in intention, the purity of her nature, reflect Hardy's own vision of her with an unequivocal clarity. But the words 'looked' and 'in her fantastic trickery' are straight from Angel's bewildered conscience. And Tess will not tell the lie – that what she has said is not true – to give him passing comfort. So great is her capacity to associate with Angel's thoughts and feelings that she remains blind to his selfishness in their crisis. Her mind, ever-active on his account to the detriment of her own, comes up with the impractical though self-sacrificial solution of divorce. We learn – for we *do* believe here – that she has always had this idea of compensation if Clare ceased to love her. While Clare's cool response is based on the law, Tess's thoughts and feelings are built on her own conception of natural justice. There is irony in the fact that justice is to be finally meted out to her in the spirit of Angel's argument – '"You don't understand the law – you don't understand!"' (p. 308). What Tess understands is beyond the law.

The death-wish finds Tess tempted to strangle herself '"with the cord of my box"' (p. 309), again prefigurative, but she does not do so because she fears that she will bring scandal on Angel's name. She follows this with the ultimate in self-immolation, the feeling that her husband should kill her. The frightful illogicality of this – the fact that he would indeed be ruined if he did – shows that Tess has lost her reason temporarily. As Douglas Brown has observed, 'The hints of madness are indecisive enough to leave a nightmare quality around her experiences.' At this stage she feels '"very greatly in the way!"' (p. 309); in fact she is, though her days are spent in loneliness and her evenings in isolation, since Angel's presence is a silent one. Signs that she is mentally unhinged by this emotionless proximity are seen when she asks if she can consider herself as his wife 'in piteous raillery' (p. 311), a phrase inserted by Hardy for the book publication of *Tess*. Insertions and analogies show Hardy's emphasis on Tess; nothing she does is 'unseemly', but the insertion before it 'quick-tempered as she naturally was' (p. 312) prepares us for her murderous quick-tempered action. This is quickly followed by the echo of the sublime words of I Cor-inthians, xiii, 5 – 'she sought not her own; was not provoked; thought no evil of his treatment of her' (p. 312). The reference to 'unseemly' and that to 'Charity' are spaced out by Hardy from the original, and serve to illustrate Tess's selflessness of spirit, which contrasts so tellingly with Angel's introverted subjectivity. Hardy was later to use the words in his poem 'The Blinded Bird'.

There is some analysis of Tess's hope that as long as she and Angel are in daily contact he may come to love her again. She is not worldly but womanly, aware of her sexuality and of the possibility of their having children. She is realist enough to know that if they emigrate there could be no disgrace but, typically, does not intrude this view upon Angel. Hardy echoes Proverbs xiv, 10, 'The intuitive heart of woman knoweth not only its own bitterness, but its husband's' (pp. 314–15), his own adaptation here focused on the extended suffering, the original being merely 'The heart knoweth his own bitterness'. The Biblical reference increases Tess's stature, but her proposal to return home is accepted by Clare almost before she has time to think it through. Once again she has made herself a victim.

The dream sequence in which Angel carries her to the stone coffin paradoxically awakens Tess's hope. The immediate effect is ironic; when he appears she immediately thinks that he has come to make love to her. The long-term effect cannot be measured, but Hardy is probing the subconscious, and the notation of what happens is bound to register profoundly with someone as sensitive as Tess. The reiteration of '"Dead! dead! dead!"' (p. 317) is a combination perhaps of regret and wish-fulfilment, but it is also an echo of her own wishes for herself. We must note Tess's fearlessness in this situation, a quality emphasized in the Stonehenge sequence: this appears to be an ironic anticipation. We also note her increasing fatalism, the omnipresence of the death-wish.

Yet her suppressed nature is cleverly released by Hardy: she luxuriates in being held and kissed (it is what she cannot have in daytime life). The self-sacrifice is complete – 'So easefully had she delivered her whole being up to him that it pleased her to think he was regarding her as his absolute possession, to dispose of as he should choose' (p. 318). Naturally in this situation she recalls that earlier carrying (in a wheelbarrow in the *Graphic*!), again emphatic of the tightness of Hardy's structure and his identification with Tess's consciousness. The death-wish predominates even in this suspended ecstasy – 'He might drown her if he would: it would be better than parting to-morrow, to lead severed lives' (p. 319). When Clare puts her down, 'Tess sat up in the coffin' (p. 320), another later insertion which looks forward imaginatively in association. The effect is somewhat Gothic, though the immediate action required is that Tess should rise from the dead in order to warm Angel into life. She ministers to him in his sleeping state, the qualities of her character – self-sacrifice and concern – apparent, for her own feet are hurt and chilled. She is inevitably over-sensitive on his account, and the next day she does not mention his sleepwalking. Tess is morally scrupulous – 'pure' – feeling that Angel may have some idea of what has happened but that he does not wish to refer to it. She imposes upon herself the penalty of silence, and as a result kills the possibility of understanding. This sensitivity helps to make her a victim.

Her brief return to Talbothays is an additional strain because she has to keep up the pretence that all is well, endure the jokes, listen to what is said about Marian and Retty. The leave-taking of the cows is sentimental and symbolic; her touching each one with her hand is a small private ritual of blessing and farewell to her happier days. The 'severity of the decree' (p. 324) that she shall not go to Angel shows that it is the woman who pays in this relationship. Tess exerts remarkable self-control and moral responsibility, for had she 'made a scene' (p. 324) Angel might have succumbed. The separation finds her 'lying in a half-dead faint' (p. 325) inside the fly: reduced by Clare's imposed coldness, Tess's own pride and obstinacy are responsible for her suffering to the last gasp of suppressed feeling.

The return – another journey, hardly a pilgrimage – is made incognito, for she learns of her marriage as retailed by the turnpike-keeper. It is a bitter irony of situation. Hearing of her father's liquid celebrations, and then having to suffer her mother's 'you little fool' (p. 328) when she confesses to having told Angel about her past, make increased anguish for Tess. More, the parental home is no longer a home for her, since her bed has been given to two younger children.

From now on emotional and economic deprivation stalk Tess, though she makes the generous gift of twenty-five pounds to help her parents; even this carries its own sadness, for she is acting from her status as a well-married woman who can afford this. She is reduced to saying 'that it was a slight return for the trouble and humiliation she had brought upon them in years past' (p. 330). Tess's pride – and Hardy uses the word 'dignity' too – is employed as an outward mask for her feelings.

Tess's absence from the action in the next two chapters does not mean that she is absent from the insistent commentary which ensures her centrality. Angel's fervid (and how ironic) assertion to his mother '"She is spotless!"' (p. 337) is defensive perhaps, but comes from a subconscious recognition of truth which he is not prepared to live by. There is Izz Huett's transcendent honesty, self-wounding, generous and forthright: '"nobody could love 'ee more than Tess did! . . . She would have laid down her life for 'ee. I could do no more"' (p. 343). In the structure of the novel Tess does just that. Her presence in her absence shows the unremitting awareness of Hardy's focus. When he returns to her (eight months have passed) the money for light dairy work and Angel's sovereigns have been eroded by the repairs to the Durbeyfield thatch. Tess's pride in adversity is now responsible for her refusal to approach Angel's parents, and she cannot return home for the same reason. Moreover, Talbothays for her is out of the question. She feels that 'her return might bring reproach upon her idolized husband. She could not have borne their pity, and their whispered remarks to one another upon her strange situation' (p. 349). She is now facing winter emotionally and physically, and she fears that Clare will not forgive her. Her plight is so bad that Hardy refers to her 'unreflecting instinct', the last word changed from the inappropriate 'automatism' of the *Graphic* version (p. 349). She has simply to concentrate on survival, but also to endure unwelcome attentions, this time from the same man who had recognized her before, fatalistically present soon in Tess's life as Farmer Groby. Close to nature herself, she flees to nature, making from the dead leaves 'a sort of nest in the middle' (p. 351). This is a deliberate reminiscence of the nest made for her by Alec on the night of her seduction, with the seasonal contrast very much in evidence. Her disturbed night reflects her disturbed life, and the death-wish returns with her own morbid intensity (and her creator's):

The wife of Angel Clare put her hand to her brow, and felt its curve, and the edges of her eye-sockets perceptible under the soft skin, and thought as she did so that a time would come when that bone would be bare. (p. 351)

38

Yet Hardy lifts her, and us, by showing her remarkable resilience and humanity. When she discovers the wounded birds Tess puts away self and weeps out her compassion 'as she killed the birds tenderly' (p. 353). The anguish and courage of this (not in the *Graphic*) show just how strong is Hardy's identification with her, as does his changing of 'hungry' to 'mangled' and 'naked' to 'bleeding' in Tess's outpouring at not suffering in the way of these creatures. Even his own anti-blood-sports attack two paragraphs earlier cannot detract from the artistic, human and humane effects of Tess's exquisitely simple action. In a simple way this is prophetic too. This is mercy killing, not murder, but it is a 'crime' of passion against man's inhumanity to creatures.

All Tess's journeys end in climactic situations of suffering or tragedy: she is inward and outward victim, but rarely numbed into acceptance. When she takes the scissors to her eyebrows the outward mutilation somehow complements the inner, and she suffers the blow to her pride when she hears herself called 'a mommet' (p. 354). The journey to Flintcomb-Ash is indicative of the bleaker isolation, inward and outward, to come. Here Hardy uses natural contrast to define Tess's suppression, her self-imposed sexless state seen against the image of the tumuli – 'as if Cybele the Many-breasted were supinely extended there' (p. 355). There is poignant pathos in her resting against the wall which 'seemed to be the only friend she had' (p. 356). Her meeting with Marian means that what she has feared – unwelcome questions – have to be answered, and Hardy stresses how the social and economic subordination of women matches the sexual one. Tess obtains work, hard though it is, for she will not cost as much to employ as a man would. Her fieldwork at Flintcomb-Ash is equivalent to her inner state. The woman pays. Tess, set off by Marian, recurs to the past of Talbothays, but there is always suffering, seen, for instance, in the irony of Tess having to hear Marian say (of her own drinking), '"You see I lost him: you didn't; and you can do without it perhaps"' (p. 362). Fortitude, patience, lingering hope, a faith in what Hardy calls 'magnanimity' (p. 362) in Angel's make-up just sustain her. Although she forbids Marian to talk of him, her own impulsive nature causes her to face 'in the direction in which she imagined South America to lie, and, putting up her lips, blew out a passionate kiss upon the snowy wind' (p. 365). Fate now closes in on Tess, with Izz and Retty arriving from one past, the Queen of Diamonds and the Queen of Spades from that other which stultifies her wifehood. With Farmer Groby there as well, she is 'like a bird caught in a clap-net' (pp. 366–7). If this is outward, the inward keeps pace with it as Marian insensitively reveals that Angel had asked Izz to go to Brazil with him. It moves her to write to Angel, and in pathetic token of her status she wears her wedding-ring all night to convince herself that she belongs to him.

The divisions and pressures within her increase. She is deeply moved by the story of Izz, and Hardy's commentary says that there 'was a limit to her powers of renunciation' (p. 371). She now convinces herself that she is guilty for not having made an approach to Angel's parents. Her fear is that either Angel is ill or indifferent to her. Her 'heart-starved situation' (p. 371) craves alleviation, but this journey is as fateful as any, with heavy symbolic accompaniment, like 'the Cross-in-Hand, where the stone pillar stands desolate and silent, to mark the site of a miracle, a murder, or both' (p. 373). Tess is socially conscious, removing her thick boots and replacing them with light, pretty ones. Ever apprehensive, fearful and superstitious, she feels that orders may have been given to refuse her admittance at the vicarage door. But Chance, that active subordinate of the greater Fate, takes her within earshot of Angel's brothers and Mercy Chant. What she overhears about herself and Angel discourages and humiliates her. The appropriation of her thick boots, the unchristian innuendo which accompanies it and her susceptible nature all combine to undermine Tess completely. She cannot bear the condemnation of Angel by his brothers. And Hardy, uncompromisingly ironic, observes that she does not know 'that the greatest misfortune of her life was this feminine loss of courage at the last and critical moment through her estimating her father-in-law by his sons' (p. 378). It is yet another might-have-been in her troubled existence.

There follows her meeting with the convert again, for she is soon aware 'that her seducer confronted her' (p. 380). This is on her return journey, with others to follow which are downhill all the way. Naturally she feels 'an almost physical sense of an implacable past which still engirdled her' (p. 385). The death-wish comes, like Alec, almost on cue – 'Bygones would never be complete bygones till she was a bygone herself' (p. 385). The irony that Alec's conversion emanates from Angel's father informs their exchanges, while Tess's social improvement is seen in his question, '"Who taught you such good English?"' (p. 389). The symbol of the 'Cross-in-Hand' is used again, and when Tess sees Izz Huett and Amby Seedling together as lovers, she feels her own deep loss.

Tess's suffering, the bleakness of her existence against the bleakest of backgrounds, is accentuated by the importunity of Alec. He produces a marriage licence (not in the *Graphic*), thus sounding one of Tess's deepest fears, namely that she is really more his wife than Angel's. Every word of Alec's injures Tess because of its implied criticism of her husband, and sometimes his directness produces an unpalatable truth, like '"You are a deserted wife, my fair Tess!"' (p. 396). It is 'almost a relief after her former experiences' (p. 397) when Groby castigates her but does not threaten her sexually. She writes to Clare but puts the letter in her box, fearing that he no longer cares for her, a feeling perhaps deriving in part from Clare's past invitation to Izz and Izz's presence at Flintcomb-Ash. Angel's influence on her is apparent: the Tess who fought for the baptism of her child now says to the sorely tempted Alec when he asks her to pray for him, '"How can I pray for you ... when I am forbidden to believe that the great Power who moves the world would alter His plans on my account?"' It is a striking statement bred from bitterness, but we might qualify it by saying that the words are uttered without sufficient preparation for the change in Tess, which has occurred off-text under the influence of Angel's views. And when she adds, '"I have been cured of the presumption of thinking otherwise,"' (p. 399) there is a feeling – perhaps only transient – that Angel's tutelage has been successful in diminishing her individuality. The texture of the statement eliminates the personal passion, and Hardy carefully emphasizes Tess's idolatry of her failed and frail Angel through Alec's cynical questioning and Tess's self-deluded '"Ah, because he knew everything!"' (p. 400). She cites chapter and verse in support of Angel's statements, innocently echoing his limitations. She is temptress despite herself, and so in love with Angel that in speaking of him (without naming him) she says, melodramatically one may feel, '"Treat him honourably – he has never wronged you! O leave his wife before any scandal spreads that may do harm to his honest name! ... A good man's honour is in my keeping – think – be ashamed!"' (pp. 402–3). Here Tess is close to stereotype and Hardy is dangerously close to bathos: his idealization of Tess is so strong that she can do no wrong except to the credibility of the reader. Her natural consistency is here lost: it returns on her next encounter with Alec, as she rests from the mechanical labour of the threshing-machine. She strikes him, driven by her familiar impetuosity to an extreme reaction.

Tess's working on the machine is physically, emotionally exhausting, and Alec sounds her vulnerability by observing, '"You are as weak as a bled calf"' (p. 415). Her response to his 'kindness' is a clutch at feeling, a craving for emotional support in this degrading void. Although Alec offers help for her family – this worked in part before and is to work again later – Tess's fear is that she will break down at the mention of her brothers and sisters. Her letter to Angel reflects the completeness of her nature – it is impassioned, informed with fear, a plea for kindness, an expression of unswerving love and a cry for help. She refers to the past as 'a dead thing altogether' (p. 417) once she had met him. The writing is unbearably poignant, for Tess's feelings have been enlarged by her suffering, her generosity of spirit and nature. And nature is the analogy she uses to stress her love and her suffering because it is lost:

'The daylight has nothing to show me, since you are not here, and I don't like to see the rooks and starlings in the fields, because I grieve and grieve to miss you who used to see them with me.' (p. 418)

The intensity of her nature, that natural poetical quality which she possesses, is here seen in exemplary expression. But the pressures are great, and we can't help feeling that hunting out Clare's favourite ballads (critics have been quick to seize on the fact that her own story is one) reflects the morbid tendency which pushes her near to madness. Hardy continues to use words like 'dream' and 'reverie' to describe her state, and she 'stood in reverie a long time' (p. 425) when Liza-Lu arrives with the news that her mother is dying.

Her journey home – again – is filled with the phases of her existence, but once arrived she shows her typical resilience and practicality. Working the allotment becomes her first resource and her major temptation when Alec makes his grotesque appearance. Always aware of the economic pressures on those closest to her, Tess is deeply moved when he offers help: 'Since returning home her soul had gone out to those children with an affection that was passionate' (p. 432). In part this is the sublimation of her feelings for Angel, but Tess has a compulsive need to give. She has no sooner recovered after making Alec angry than she is overturned by unexpected family fate – her mother recovers, her father dies. Economic deprivation, family displacement because he only held the tenure of the cottage for his lifetime, these combine to place Tess within the orbit of Alec's emotional blackmail with greater risk.

Hardy's social and moral commentary on change provides the foreground to Tess's increased suffering, with the village community and its narrow standards *vis-à-vis* Tess's past satirized ('By some means the village had to be kept pure,' p. 436.) The pure woman pays again, blaming herself, as she did over Prince, for her family's plight. If she had not come back they might have survived within the community sympathy; but she tends her baby's grave, and is therefore an ostentatious sinner, inviting victimization. 'Reverie' frequently overtakes her now. She hardly notices Alec when he comes to see her: '"I heard you, I believe, though I fancied it was a carriage and horses. I was in a sort of dream"' (p. 437). Her association is with her wedding and Angel's telling her of the legend; it shows her ever-present and natural morbid tendency to look back, but there is a hint too, I feel, that she is becoming unstable. Alec's story of the legend is yet another prophetic structure and a further undermining of her resistance when he reiterates his offer of help for her family.

She resists and writes an impassioned, poignant note to Angel accusing him of treating her badly. Obsessed with her situation, seeing what she believes is the true morality of it, she begins to feel that Alec takes precedence over Angel: 'Yet a consciousness that in a physical sense this man alone was her husband seemed to weigh on her more and more' (p. 442). There is no doubt that Hardy is intent on stressing this obsession. The sentence did not appear in the *Graphic*, but Hardy's insertion shows that Tess's mental and emotional judgement has been warped by the immediate pressures and Angel's silence.

The 'house-ridding' journey is as fateful as any Tess undertakes. Hardy establishes their disadvantaged situation – 'They were only women . . . hence they had to hire a waggon at their own expense, and got nothing sent gratuitously' (p. 443). The meeting with Izz and Marian, the sheltering in the d'Urberville vault, her mother's plaintive recriminations – '"O Tess, what's the use of your playing at marrying gentlemen, if it leaves us like this!"' (p. 447) – are all contributory factors in her reduction. Alec's trick of lying on the altar tomb shakes and shocks her, and the location ensures that the death-wish returns with powerful anguish as she says at the entrance to the vaults, '"Why am I on the wrong side of this door!"' (p. 449). And unbeknown to her Izz and Marian have contributed their mite to Tess's fate by writing in a generous-spirited but warning manner to Angel.

The meshes which enwrap Tess draw tighter in the throbbing ironies of the final phase, 'Fulfilment'. With the switch of focus to Angel at the beginning Hardy compounds the irony of the situation by keeping Tess in the forefront of our minds. The quotations from the letter convey her anguish: '"I must cry to you in my trouble – I have no one else . . . I think I must die if you do not come soon . . . If you will send me one little line and say, *I am coming soon*, I will bide on, Angel, O so cheerfully!"' (p. 456).

Narrative tension is generated as Angel seeks Tess. The Sandbourne lodging-house scene underlines why Hardy originally had 'Too Late, Beloved' as a title choice. Tess's extreme suffering on seeing him makes her utter the words 'Too late' four times in agonized response to his tenderness. At this moment of crisis Hardy maintains his consistency of presentation. As she speaks to Angel we are told that 'She seemed to feel like a fugitive in a dream, who tries to move away but cannot' (p. 466). This is like – but with a difference – her self-absorption in other crises, and the difference lies in the strong suggestion of guilt and instability. Her direct, frank acknowledgement that she is d'Urberville's mistress was not in the *Graphic* version, for its readership was not prepared to accept such phrases as 'He is upstairs' and 'I didn't care what he did wi' me!' (pp. 466–7). Thereafter the broken words of the broken girl, her mind shattered by the emaciated Angel she has just seen, convey her anguish and move her to impetuous murder – wish-fulfilment, consummation after betrayal. When she overtakes Angel we see how aware she is of her own nature and its movement of aggression as the only *fulfilment* possible to her. As she says, '"I feared long ago, when I struck him on the mouth with my glove, that I might do it some day for the trap he set me in my simple youth"' (p. 474). This kind of self-knowledge is quickly obscured by her impossible reasoning over what she has done. And here, I suggest, Hardy's insights and subtlety of presentation achieve a remarkable closeness of identification with his heroine. The signs of mental and emotional instability are clearly indicated, and Hardy, mindful always of her purity, expresses them as the natural consequences of the fateful pressures to which she has been subjected. Take these words:

'– Why did you go away – why did you – when I loved you so? I can't think why you did it . . . Angel, will you forgive me my sin against you, now I have killed him?' (p. 474)

The questions show clearly the state of Tess's mind. To the first question, in her sane state, Tess knows the answer. To the second she doesn't, and for the simple reason that the sane Tess knows the difference between right and wrong. Of all the crises she suffers, the return of Angel is the greatest and Hardy, accused of melodramatics over the murder by some critics, identifies his heroine's hysteria and the pathos of her questions with an unerring focus. Tess cannot be rational here, and there is the notation of her self-absorption which we have noticed so often. When Angel questions her about the killing of Alec, her response is '"I mean that I have,"' *she murmured in a reverie*' (p. 474). The italics are mine. This is the symptom of her abstraction, her withdrawal from reality. The broken words are a kind of articulated reverie, a reflex statement of her inward feelings. Although Angel feels that her love for him 'had apparently extinguished her moral sense altogether'

(p. 475), Tess thinks that she has acted in a moral sense, a sense of justice which her tortured mind is implementing. Further evidence for her unbalanced state of mind is that once she is reunited with Angel he appears to her unchanged – 'To her he was, as of old, all that was perfection' (p. 475). Of even greater significance at this juncture is Hardy's use of the word which defines his conception of Tess. To her Angel has 'the face of the one man on earth who had loved her purely, and who had believed in her as pure' (p. 475–6). And even in his physical identifications of Tess Hardy maintains the consistency of an integrated psychology. Released from Alec, reunited with Angel, Tess's reaction is physical as well as emotional. '"I feel strong enough to walk any distance," said she' (p. 477), a natural resilience again being part of her character; it makes her coming death all the more poignant, she is so full of vital health.

She and Angel stay in the deserted mansion for five days, with Tess unwilling to move, wanting to stretch out this 'fulfilment'. As she says, '"All is trouble outside there; inside here content"' (p. 481). But Tess is always true to herself: she is as always insecure, self-condemnatory, apprehensive, seeing only a temporary happiness:

'I fear that what you think of me now may not last. I do not wish to outlive your present feeling for me. I would rather not. I would rather be dead and buried when the time comes for you to despise me, so that it may never be known to me that you despised me.' (p. 481)

This is transcendent, bleak, hopeless, brave; it does not arise from being instructed in philosophy or religion, or as a result of Clare's tutelage. It comes from a life experience which has been savage and wounding. Tess's fatalism is not a creed: it is a personal, moral, social, economic and spiritual fact. Consistent and complex, she is born to suffer, but suffering, as we saw from the baptism of Sorrow, irradiates and elevates her in the flesh and the spirit, as here.

The Stonehenge sequence presents Tess as symbol, with that forecasting element so often present in the structure employed here with imminent, intimate association. We remember Angel in the sleepwalking sequence placing her in the stone coffin: here she places herself on the sacrificial slab. Her generosity of spirit embraces Liza-Lu and Clare, yet another facet of sacrifice. And here again she is natural and wrongheaded at the same time. Liza-Lu, she observes, is '"so good and simple and *pure*"' (p. 485), my italics again. She continues to urge Clare, telling him that '"People marry sister-in-laws continually about Marlott"', and adding that he should '"train her and teach her, Angel, and bring her up for your own self"' (p. 485). There is deep pathos here, a sense of pathetically ensuring that Clare gets what he wants from life and that Liza-Lu subserves him as Tess has and would have continued to do in life. It is a kind of living on. Liza-Lu would be economically saved, educationally lifted, domestically moulded. If the woman has paid, the man will still rule. So pure and essentially simple is Tess that her experience has taught her nothing beyond the misplaced dependence which has contributed to her tragedy. This unselfishness, which is an aberration, is combined with that superstitious, religious sense that she will be fated beyond the grave, that she will not see him, accepting his silence as negation of what she wants – '"And I wanted to see you again – so much, so much! What – not even you and I, who love each so well?"' (p. 486). We should ponder on the words which convey the ironic sense of Tess's delusion about Angel and his pervasive knowledge. And her obsession is registered in her '"This happiness could not have lasted. It was too much. I have had enough: and now I shall not live for you to despise me!"' This is her small fulfilment, the words reflecting Tess's fear of the conventional laws which have dominated her life. Tess, who has been vibrant with life, has from the beginning been shadowed by death.

2. The Other Characters

If Tess occupies the foreground of our responses and concerns, the other characters are not lacking in interest or individuality, though some tend to be mainly functional. In presenting two contrasting temperaments, those of the sensual Alec d'Urberville and the intellectual Angel Clare, Hardy employs his basic structure of natural contrast. He imposes personality on what could so easily be stereotype. For example, Alec with his 'mistarshers' seems on first acquaintance to be the staple, single-dimensioned villain of Victorian melodrama. Angel, with his rejection of conventional faith, could so conveniently be registered as an ironically presented type of the period. But neither fits his own stereotype, for circumstances show them developing beyond it, although, because of the centrality of Tess, neither is seen completely in the round. Each is flesh and symbol, complementing the other in the fall and rise and rise and fall again of Tess herself. In simple terms, Alec is not all bad and Angel is not all good, even before his inability to accept Tess's confession. In both Hardy is presenting, I suggest, male dominance, with the resulting reduction of the woman, in the flesh or the spirit or both. Alec is predatory in the flesh, Angel in the spirit, though there is some overlap in each case. It is perhaps initially difficult to think of Angel as being sexually jealous, but a close look at his reactions shows Hardy underlining his slavery to the code of masculine conventional response to transgression in the woman. The man indulges and at best repents: the woman pays.

If each man is seen in contrast to the other, both are seen in contrast to Tess. She is seen in her fullness of nature, and by a cunning obliquity Hardy presents in Angel and Alec each side of her nature deliberately distorted. Alec's lust and sensuality, animalism if you like, are cleverly and distortingly mirrored in Tess's natural affection, warmth and passionate feelings. Angel's rational intellectualism, abstract and depersonalized, is distortingly reflected in Tess's mysticism, absorption (reverie) and natural poetry. And both men are seen almost exclusively in relation to her. Because of this, I feel, Hardy does not present them fully: the other elements of their personalities are to be found in the margins of the narrative. The decisions which make Alec a hell-fire preacher and Angel an agnostic, though given in retrospect, are only present in the narrative as results rather than causes. Hardy shows them in interaction with Tess (second time around with Alec) when their main bias is set. The interconnection is also present in their relations with Tess. Alec does not wish to discard her – she insists on going home – but when she comes into his life again he refuses to give her up. His presents first-time around, easy blandishments from a practised hand, become a home for Tess's family and a lodging-house in Sandbourne for his mistress later. This contrasts curiously with Angel's 'possession' of Tess, his unphysical but mental and emotional domination of her at Talbothays, his hold over her despite his rejection of her confession, his fulfilment in the deserted mansion after the murder of Alec, his (possibly) continued possession of her in Liza-Lu. The contrast is worked on a number of levels: for example, Alec abuses Tess in the flesh and Angel in the spirit, but even more cunning is the fact that Alec's condemnation of Tess's husband finds its equivalent in Angel's unspoken condemnation of Tess's seducer, who has changed his image of Tess. Both men are integral to Tess's experience, just as both are integral to Hardy's artistic structure.

Angel appears first, fleetingly, in Tess's life, his distance from her and what she represents perhaps prefiguring his later distance both physically in Brazil and mentally in his emotional incapacity. His passing response to her is quickly dismissed, this reflex showing his turn for rational decision. This first glimpse shows Hardy's concern to give him a consistency of stance. The next at Talbothays is registered through Tess's appraisal that despite his 'local livery' there is 'something educated, reserved, subtle, sad, differing' (p. 166). Nominally this is Tess's judgement, but the words are too sophisticated for her. It is Hardy defining him as Tess's memory works over his appearance and recalls him as the passing stranger.

Hardy's introduction of him is deliberate and formalized, and Clare's own language in rejection of the Church is formalized too. It is almost the language of the preacher turned anti-preacher: '"I cannot honestly be ordained her minister, as my brothers are, while she refuses to liberate her mind from an untenable redemptive theolatry"' (p. 170). The last clause was not in the *Graphic*, understandably so in view of its sentiments. But the statement is pompous and stiff – Angel is self-conscious and pronounces on things great and small with some pedantry. But we feel Hardy's voice within Angel as well, particularly when he observes that his education would not be for the 'honour and glory of God', but of man (p. 171). Angel, however, is not lacking in feeling (we may think his brothers are), for he is made quite ill by seeing his father's suffering over his (Angel's) heresy.

Apart from the retrospect, and an unconvincingly interpolated scene in Brazil, we see Angel in interaction with Tess. He is late (aged twenty-six) in fixing on farming as a career, feels that it will give him 'intellectual liberty' (p. 172) and likes the outdoor life for its own sake. His early idealizing of Tess does not prevent Hardy from preparing us for his moral stance and demanding standard. Tess herself initially regards 'Angel Clare as an intelligence rather than as a man' (p. 181), but the intelligent man here does not know himself. Often the ideal and the personal reveal his inconsistency. This is seen in his radical attitude towards old families which breaks down at the idea of his marrying the descendant of one and thus compensating by her ancestry for her lack of status. Hardy is here focusing convincingly on an aspect of human nature common to so many of us: between the ideal and its practice falls the shadow of reality. Clare before he knows of her family inheritance idealizes her by literary analogy – she is 'Artemis, Demeter' and a 'visionary essence of woman' (p. 187). That he thinks in analogy is a further hint of his incapacity to experience adversity, or to enter into a fullness of life which will not admit of being categorized. The incident which was not included in the *Graphic* because of its explicitness shows him picking up Tess after having carried the other three girls through the water, and whispering to her '"Three Leahs to get one Rachel"' (p. 202). The effect of such a comparison, ready to hand, is to distance him from life, and even in commentary there is the same diminishing emphasis. Consider this: 'He had never before seen a woman's lips and teeth which forced upon his mind with such persistent iteration the old Elizabethan simile of roses filled with snow' (p. 209). Literature is not life but a representation of it, and references like this constitute an ironic comment on Clare and his stance towards Tess. In his idealization of her he sees her as an extension of his own culture rather than as a woman. His instructing, educating, moulding is designed in fact to re-create her in his image. He has importunate moments, but his conscience and a certain sexual scrupulosity inhibit much natural expression. Hardy also subdues Clare to a functional consistency. The *Graphic*'s 'continually burning to be with her; driven by every impulse within him' becomes in revision the less physical 'driven towards her by every heave of his pulse' (p. 215).

Clare is presented very much as the man of his time who is protector and instructor, since his wife-to-be is his social inferior. His sincerity in relation to Tess is unquestionable – he believes that 'It was for herself that he loved Tess' (p. 226). In fact his blindness lies in part within himself, and also in his inability to hear her confession early in their love. Once or twice he succumbs to her physicality, but generally his wooing is with words. His learning that she is a d'Urberville is an unlooked for bonus, for he can be enlightened and radical at the same time. Yet his wish to hasten their marriage suggests a deep-rooted insecurity, something which is to be brought into the open when he learns about Tess's past. As Hardy puts it, 'He loved her dearly, though perhaps rather ideally and fancifully' (p. 269). He passes through the fateful incidents – the Trantridge man recognizing Tess, for example – innocently oblivious, his own course of action predetermined, even to the insensitivity of failing to tell Tess why the banns were not published and, specifically and fatally, his choice of the d'Urberville farmhouse for their honeymoon. This is meant as a compliment to Tess, but it is at once a reminder of her past and displays a false pride in her ancestry. He is alternately sensitive and obtuse, obstinate. His blunders are the worst part of Tess's suffering before her revelation, and although they are inadvertent they reflect the inadequacies of this enlightened man.

After the revelation, the inadequacy, the inability to get outside the narrow compass of self, is exposed. Hitherto Hardy has presented Angel as a somewhat oblique or distant character, but in adversity he is given a much fuller presentation. Here Hardy is presenting him as confused, stricken, trying to be generous in spirit and not succeeding. He is given greater substance and, although our sympathies are with Tess, he is not without some share of our compassion. His coldness to her, his moments of indecision where we feel he *might* sustain their marriage, and above all the dream sequence with Hardy's telling revelations of the conflict in his subconscious – all this shows him to be a suffering, developing character. He continues to blunder and offend, stating the man's rights with unthinking insensitivity: '"I thought – any man would have thought – that by giving up all ambition to win a wife with social standing, with fortune, with knowledge of the world, I should secure rustic innocence as surely as I should secure pink cheeks"' (p. 308). Although Tess feels for his position keenly, sympathetically here, we can't: the implication of woman as possession or subordinate is too strong, too condescending, to be anything but abhorrent. His self-control, moral discipline, capacity for obstinate resistance, the withdrawal into himself, all these show Clare's strength of character built on an inflexible egoism. Hardy refers to the 'hard logical deposit' (p. 311) which is buried in his nature. Yet we should be wary of judging him too harshly. Like Tess, and the comparison is a valid one, I think, he is divided against himself. He tells her that she is his wife not his servant, says that she is respectable, and obstinately rests his attitude and behaviour on a principle. He resists her obvious physical appeal by not kissing her, and then wishes that he had. This is symptomatic of his divisions, for he recognizes that Alec (as yet unnamed) is '"your husband in Nature, and not I"' (p. 313). This is an echo of Tess's own feelings and, since she reveres what Angel says, has doubtless some influence in driving her finally towards Alec. It is Clare who lays down the conditions of their parting (is she his wife or his servant?). The rules are made by the man – '"there is that which I cannot endure at present"' (p. 324) – and Tess is bound to keep them. She can write, but she cannot go to him. Clare though has his own struggle – 'He wondered if he had treated her unfairly' (p. 333) before *impetuously* deciding to go to Brazil. Hardy makes it clear that Angel's own tragedy lies in the fact that he hardly realizes that he loves Tess. His impassioned '"She is spotless!"' (p. 337) in response to his mother's questioning shows the depth of his feelings, his loyalty, and his pride, and also his inability to translate them into direct and warm communication with his wife.

The divisions and insecurity are shown in two incidents before he departs. The first is when he whispers heterodox ideas to Mercy Chant (is Angel too a little unbalanced in his extremity?): afterwards he says '"... you must forgive me. I think I am going crazy!"' (p. 340). The second is his *impetuous* invitation to Izz Huett to accompany him to Brazil, and his retraction of it when Izz tells him that Tess's love was greater than anyone else's could be. Once again it seems that Hardy is indicating a pattern of contrasts with Tess: Angel's irrationality here shows him emotionally unbalanced. The revelation has been too much for both of them.

In a curious way both incidents humanize Angel. The 'hard logical deposit' has its own soft centre, and when he returns to kneel at the forsaken bedside he is crying, his words reflecting a blindness which he doesn't even suspect – '"O Tess! If you had only told me sooner. I would have forgiven you!"' (p. 341). This is the duplicity of hindsight, an extension of his irrationality, a pathetic belief that he would have had a different attitude towards his wife's 'sin'. After his parting from Izz we are told that he was 'within a feather-weight's turn of abandoning his road to the nearest station' (p.345). But he doesn't (another tantalizing might-have-been). Angel, chained to principle, still thinking himself right, continues wrong-headed and wrong-hearted to put distance between himself and Tess.

From then on we only get glimpses of Angel until his return, though he is omnipresent in Tess's consciousness. He ages in terms of mental and emotional maturity, though we are not shown it in process. It is complemented by his physical deterioration. In Brazil he accepts the words of a stranger, and 'from being her critic he grew to be her advocate' (p. 423). It is 'too late beloved'. When he comes back he makes his fateful journey of discovery over Tess's terrain. His meeting with Tess shows him bewildered and anguished and, afterwards, uncertain that Tess has killed Alec. In their few precious days together Angel's love, his tenderness, his compassion, the solicitude he shows for her, now unprotected and vulnerable, show that his life experience has given him the capacity to change. He is almost ennobled by the experiences, but Tess is the focus of our interest and sympathy. Clare represents the personal tragedy of those who think they are enlightened until something which affects them occurs and drives a wedge of doubt and rejection into their minds. Clare thinks that he has mastered, got into perspective, the conventions and pettinesses of his time. He hasn't: he lacks magnanimity, particularly of action, so that a spontaneous burst of affection is rare. His animation is low, he sees largely what he wants to see, he is obdurate until life ruins his health and he has time to look back in anguish. His real goodness takes too much time to surface, though his moral awareness and self-questioning (and self-suffering) show his innate movement towards the positive enlightenment which has eluded him in his love for Tess.

Angel is mainly mind, Alec mainly flesh. Alec's functional role is clear. He is tempted, ravishes Tess, disdains her when she leaves to return home, is converted after his brush with Angel's father, is once more tempted by Tess, tempts her by his provision for her family, makes her his mistress and is murdered by her. I give this bald summary because the outline is that of the sensation novel of the period, a Victorian melodrama rather than a tragedy. But Hardy transforms his material by a deepening ironic contemplation of Alec, who moves from the indolent self-gratification to persuasive, emotional blackmail and a kind of loving in his relations with Tess. The irony is sustained on a number of levels. For instance, there is the failure of the enlightened man, Angel, to express his enlightenment in broad acceptance and love, and the success of the failed convert, Alec, to reduce Tess by relieving the needs of her family. The fake d'Urberville possesses the real d'Urberville as a result. Alec is initially seen posing, a stereotype whose function is to seduce the heroine: under Hardy's hands he develops into the man who renounces the flesh and then finds that it is too much for him. If Alec's conversion is not completely convincing, his renunciation of the spirit in his reawakened lust for Tess is immediate, opportunist, cunning. The fact that he and Angel complement one another is underlined in every phase of the action. Alec returns, Angel does not (until too late); Alec in Tess's mind (reinforced by Angel's) is her real husband, while Angel, who marries her, is not and does not consummate the marriage (or if he does, not until too late); Angel has no knowledge of or interest in Tess's family, whereas Alec gives them some degree of comfort. Symbolically, they are given distinct Biblical associations, with Alec appearing at the allotment bonfire as Devil, and Angel looking like 'Crivelli's dead *Christus*' (p. 454) on his return. Alec's determination is one of his main qualities, linked to sadistic actions at times. He forces the strawberry into Tess's mouth, enjoys breaking his horse after nearly being broken by it himself and gives Tess 'the kiss of mastery' (p. 96) which indicates that he will succeed in making her his mistress. He tries all manner of persuasion, reverting to stereotype when he uses phrases like 'my Beauty', but coming back into normal orbit when he tells her that he has given her father a new cob and the children some toys. Alec is clever and generous, because he can afford to be and it is the way of his world. And when Tess leaves him some weeks after the seduction we are aware of her pride and shame but also of his easy reflex of giving. He says, '"You know you need not work in the fields or the dairies again. You know you may clothe yourself with the best, instead of in the bald plain way you have lately affected"' (p. 125). This has curious associations with Angel's leaving Tess what seem adequate funds, and of Tess being forced to work after each encounter with a man. Alec and Angel, as I have indicated, represent complementary halves of the human personality, and the structural patterning of contrast is insistent. Nominally Angel is a 'better' man than Alec, yet 'better' lends itself to negations. In relation to both men, Tess is in each case a victim. The marked difference is in Alec's degree of self-knowledge – '"I was born bad, and I have lived bad, and I shall die bad in all probability"' (p. 125). He even has the forethought to say to Tess 'if certain circumstances should arise' (p. 125) he will provide for her, a direct acknowledgement that she may be pregnant. There is regret too on his part when she goes: '"And yet, Tess, will you come back to me? Upon my soul, I don't like to let you go like this!"' (p. 127). The 'me' here which replaced the 'Trantridge' of the *Graphic* version shows Hardy subtly deepening Alec's *personal* feeling for Tess: in a way, it even prepares us for the backsliding of the convert.

Nothing prepares us for the convert himself. For a long period Alec is as absent from the plot as Angel is from Tess. His return is just as much a stereotype as his early outline. And just as he did earlier, Hardy almost diminishes Alec by the abundant detail of his descriptions: 'the former curves of sensuousness were now modulated to lines of devotional passion. The lip-shapes that had meant seductiveness were now made to express supplication . . . animalism had become fanaticism' (p. 383). And so on. But the new Alec is the old Alec and the 'transfiguration', as Hardy calls it, is skin-deep. He delights in '"having a good slap at yourself"' (p. 387), but this indicates the extremes of self-indulgence or self-denial which mark his emotional boundaries. From then on that determination which I stressed earlier, allied to the resources he has at his command, establishes his 'mastery' over Tess again. He has an incisive ability to utter insidious truths, like '"I see you are in a bad way – neglected by one who ought to cherish you"' (p. 410). Alternately grotesque and persuasive, importunate and passionate, d'Urberville has developed greater fluency since his conversion. In Angel's absence, it tells. If Angel represents romance, Alec represents fleshly realism: he is so taken with Tess sexually that he determines to possess her regardless of her inward feelings. The inward Tess remains shut off from him, just as the inward Tess was unknown to Angel.

If the male protagonists dominate her life in different ways, Tess's family, in its economic and domestic and newly acquired ancestry, dominates her in another. They constitute her small world until she goes to Trantridge, and that world is largely represented by the often-tipsy and indolent Sir John and his ever-oppressed, irresponsible but resilient wife. If the d'Urbervilles are debased, the Durbeyfield parents represent the extreme effects. Hardy's lesser characters are often seen naturally against their place and time and the conditions which have made them. They are true and functional in social context; the Durbeyfields are feckless and, in Joan's case at least, opportunistic. They are fatalistic, and just as Tess is a victim, so they are victims too – in their case not so much of their debased inheritance, which they have been ignorant of anyway, but of their debased existence, an economic–agricultural deprivation which has certainly helped to make them what they are. Hardy is much concerned with the effects of nature and nurture, and John and Joan Durbeyfield are the result of both. If they are seen as economic and moral reality, they are also seen and felt verbally, the authenticating reality of speech making them individuals, not caricature. The father's world is largely encompassed by The Pure Drop and Rolliver's, Joan's by the uplift of an excursion to join him as an escape from the weekly sea of washing. Their improvidence springs in part from drink: Tess's being the only member of the family who can take the beehives to Casterbridge sets the tragedy in motion. Sir John digs a grave for Prince, though he has failed to grow any crops for his family and, later on, they are reduced to eating their own seed potatoes. Improvidence is therefore seen as the recourse of people who have been so reduced that they no longer have the will to rise above their bare subsistence level. They accept what comes their way, and Parson Tringham's revelation confers upon Durbeyfield the excuse he needs to continue in indolence though he hasn't the means to afford it. He can boast of his 'family' to his drinking companions. Hardy presents the Durbeyfields with a mixture of ironic criticism and pathetic/comic innuendo. The scenes of the family interior, infinitely depressing and lowering, are some of Hardy's best, mainly because of the complete identification with place and character which he achieves. Take our first sight and sounds of Joan – '"God bless thy diment eyes! And thy waxen cheeks! And thy cherry mouth! And thy Cubit's thighs! And every bit o' thy blessed body!"' (p. 57). It is a simple expression of love 'in the muck and muddle of rearing children' (p. 60). Hardy gives man and wife a natural consistency, so that we can accept the debased compatibility, the ever-increasing family, Joan's conditioned closing of her eyes to her husband's faults and their joint apathy over the lifehold tenancy. Durbeyfield's assumption of pride in the family is a cover for a permanent debility of character. Though he affects to be sensitive about Tess going to Trantridge, he is too self-absorbed to show her any warmth of feeling when she goes. Joan is the prime mover, alive to the economic and status possibilities in the situation. Joan thinks ahead to some recompense for Tringham, who has put them in the way of upward mobility and Hardy superbly integrates a natural comic touch into their unchanged lives by Sir John's offering to sell his title for £1,000, subsequently reduced to £20. Yet Joan, once Tess has gone, shows she has a heart and a conscience, and something of the worrying nature which characterizes her daughter – '"I was thinking that perhaps it would ha' been better if Tess had not gone"' (p. 93). It is an acknowledgement of her ambition on her daughter's account and an admission in spirit of the risks involved. She does not need the prevision of *The Compleat Fortune-Teller* to underline the fact that she may have sacrificed her daughter.

Hardy shows, given the family circumstances, their degree of resilience, a quality we have noted in Tess herself. Joan accepts what has happened to Tess – pregnancy without marriage – with the fatalism which is her daily survival kit. She is subdued, perhaps made to feel guilty (she is not insensitive) by Tess's accusatory '"Why didn't you tell me there was a danger in men-folk?"' (p. 131). Sir John, his new status part of his consciousness, is more aware of the shame that Tess has brought on the family, so much so that he refuses to let the parson visit the house when Tess needs him. The economic trap which encloses the family ensures that Tess continues to be vulnerable, for Joan's advice to her not to tell her young man of her past trouble arises from the fact that Tess married will probably be able to make some provision for them. Joan is strongly individualized here, with the letter written in the third person, the irony covering the lack of education and the subterfuge which Joan is employing as a parent with the moral authority to dictate the advice. The hypocrisy and self-interest disgust Tess. When she writes again it is natural that she receives no reply from Joan, for her mother believes that her face is her fortune. Yet when Angel calls on her to discover Tess's whereabouts, her conscience, or her sense of romance, or both, asserts itself at the critical moment. Pressed by Clare she speaks out, but not before she has reprimanded him:

'Do you think that Tess would wish me to try and find her? If not, of course –'
   'I don't think she would.'
   'Are you sure?'
   'I am sure she wouldn't.'
   He was turning away; and then he thought of Tess's tender letter.
   'I am sure she would!' he retorted passionately. 'I know her better than you do.'
   'That's very likely, sir; for I have never really known her.'
   'Please tell me her address, Mrs Durbeyfield, in kindness to a lonely wretched man!'
   Tess's mother again restlessly swept her cheek with her vertical hand, and seeing that he suffered, she at last said, in a low voice –
   'She is at Sandbourne.' (pp. 461–2)

I give this exchange because it shows how carefully Hardy captures the natural temper and tension of the interaction, and because Mrs Durbeyfield has developed a kind of sobriety in keeping with her withdrawn and secure status. Note the admission (true, since she has not known Tess in the sense of understanding her), and the combination of warmth, irresponsibility and compassion which leads her to reveal, in general terms, where Tess is. Here the realistic and the functional are seen together: Joan becomes the unwitting agent of Tess's last tragedy. In *Tess*, as in all his major fiction, Hardy's subordinate characters are drawn from the life he knew. They are observed, transformed with artistic certainty, and presented with realistic force and functional relevance.

Outside the Durbeyfield family – Abraham and Liza-Lu are sketchily but convincingly particularized – Hardy takes observed traits, responses and actions, bringing character alive by the simple expedient of making what is shown so recognizable and natural that what is not shown is felt and known without need for comment. Izz, Marian and Retty are individualized in this way: we see them in interaction with each other, with Tess, with Angel, with Dairyman Crick and his wife. They too are real and functional. They stand in contradistinction to Tess, since they are milkmaids and field-women without the spiritual, imaginative or sexual qualities possessed by Tess. They are not beautiful or educated: they are variously romantic, silly, sentimental, tipsy, sad, confiding, jealous, to name but a few of the personal traits described. Functionally they exist as a chorus to Tess's affair with Clare: individually they exist as typical of their time and of all time. Their reactions to Tess's marrying Clare are perhaps overdone, but in that superb sequence at Talbothays where they languish for Angel, Hardy prepares the way for their later hysteria:

The air of the sleeping-chamber seemed to palpitate with the hopeless passion of the girls. They writhed feverishly under the oppressiveness of an emotion thrust on them by cruel Nature's law – an emotion which they had neither expected nor desired. The incident of the day had fanned the flame that was burning the inside of their hearts out, and the torture was almost more than they could endure. (p. 204)

Angel carrying each one through the flood is an opportunity for pathetic self-indulgence: for that passing moment each one has him. Retty's neurosis deepens, Marian takes to drink, while Izz suffers worst of all, though generosity of spirit forces her to acknowledge that Tess's love is greater than her own. There is a postscript to the relationship with Tess. Marian and Izz as 'two well-wishers' write to Angel, showing that the warmth of friendship which subsisted at Talbothays and Flintcomb-Ash was not merely passing. This is slight in terms of characterization, positive in terms of reality.

Another aspect of Hardy's characterization is his ability to bring to life the character who enters the action and leaves it without more than a transitory functional role, if that. Consider the natural observation in the presentation of characters as widely apart sympathetically as Tess's brother Abraham and the Queens of Diamonds and Spades. His appraisal of Abraham captures the child's imaginative predilections, giving the starting-point of what he has overheard. The precocity of Abraham is conveyed with natural understanding and a fine ear: Abraham is innocent, his innocence complementing Tess's, and his anguish over Prince is a mirror of hers. But like so many of Hardy's characters he is real as well as functional, and his exchange with Tess about the stars (pp. 69–70), though central to the fatalistic theme, is not arbitrarily imposed. It grows out of the inquiring mind which wants knowledge but has little wider chance of getting it. It grows out of character in the particular situation: the insights conveyed by Tess's replies are balanced by the insights into the child, who has worked out what must happen if their blighted lot is to be improved. The dialogue is natural, easy, but charged: Abraham wants to be told the story of other worlds, and the novel is centrally about his sister and her story in this 'blighted' world. A few words have brought Abraham alive and at the same time pointed his relevance in the artistic structure of the novel.

A completely contrasting scene is that involving Car Darch and her crew, who are brought to life with a sudden eruptive force: there is a like immediacy of truth. Car Darch has the accident with the treacle which brings down ridicule upon herself. In words and action the scene reflects the major contrast between the Queen of Spades and Tess, who has had the unthinking temerity to laugh with the rest:

'How darest th' laugh at me, hussy!' she cried.

'I couldn't really help it when t'others did,' apologized Tess, still tittering.

'Ah, th'st think th' beest everybody, dostn't, because th' beest first favourite with He just now! But stop a bit, my lady, stop a bit! I'm as good as two of such! Look here – here's at 'ee!'

To Tess's horror the dark queen began stripping off the bodice of her gown – which for the added reason of its ridiculed condition she was only too glad to be free of – till she had bared her plump neck, shoulders, and arms to the moonshine, under which they looked as luminous and beautiful as some Praxitilean creation, in their possession of the faultless rotundities of a lusty country girl. She closed her fists and squared up to Tess. (pp. 111–12).

Hardy's presentation here is achieved with a striking awareness of life and art. The scene is vibrant with reality, with the crude sensuality and jealousy, prelude to violence, but the comparison with the artist underlines Hardy's own art. These are country girls, one here being compared with artistic beauty as revealed in classical antiquity. Hardy is deliberately using the analogy to indicate that ugly realism – violence, coarseness – is sometimes found with outward physical beauty which artists strive to capture. The Queen of Spades's Amazonian qualities are stressed. She is life and larger than life, and the scene is rich in humour and grotesque effects created by the moonlight, and also because most of the company have been drinking. It shows Hardy's attention to detail in character, and this continues when Alec picks up Tess and gallops off with her. Character becomes chorus, but with no loss of identity: as dark Car's mother observes, '"Out of the frying-pan into the fire"' (p. 113). The omniscient irony is reinforced by the unpleasant cackle of truth.

Passing or minor characters are integrated into the action as here: they are part of the naturalistic force which carries Tess along, their lives ignorant and uncomprehending. Once again they are at the lowest end of the economic structure of this rural society. At the end of this scene Hardy refers to their 'erratic motions' (p. 113). It is a phrase which summarizes their lives. Others are more structural than earthy, like the painter of biblical texts, whose warnings in red letters are applicable to Tess, and whose wanderings somehow reflect the fateful journeys of Tess herself. Her first meeting with him is the most significant, subserving as it does the themes of fate and guilt. The Christian in him helps Tess carry her basket as she returns pregnant from Trantridge. But when she asks him about inadvertent sin he replies that he cannot split hairs. Then he goes on:

'But you should read my hottest ones – them I kips for slums and seaports. They'd make you wriggle! Not but what this is a very good tex for rural districts ... Ah! – there's a nice bit of blank wall up by that barn standing to waste. I must put one there – one that it will be good for dangerous young females like yourself to heed. Will ye wait, missy?' (p. 128).

He then proceeds to paint 'THOU, SHALT, NOT, COMMIT – (p. 129) before referring Tess 'for edification' to 'Mr Clare of Emminster' (p. 129). Apart from acting as a sounding-board for Tess's conscience, the painter of texts subserves other functions in Hardy's interactive character-structure. He is part of the patterning which links Tess with the Clares before she is related to them by marriage. His advice that she should consult Mr Clare is ironic in view of Tess's later journey to Emminster, which proves to be abortive. These are part of the structural symmetry, but there is further the painter's own sanctimonious certainty of tone – an extremity which provokes rebellion from Tess. His delight – look at 'hottest' and 'wriggle' – has a self-satisfaction which anticipates that of Alec later in his new-found if temporary conversion. This passing character exults at the thought of making sinners pay, a sadistic streak evident in his reference to 'dangerous young females'. By counterpointing this with Alec's later hell-fire delivery, Hardy is demonstrating through character the nature of a religiosity which takes over individuals and conditions their lives. Even allowing for Hardy's particular bias, there is a truth here which again gives the individual a wide currency: we recognize the type.

The religious individual is a favourite area of concern for Hardy in *Tess*, from this painter and the clergyman whose inadequacy is shown to Tess, to Alec in passing and the Clare family in essence. Cuthbert and Felix are seen satirically and historically (remember our first sight of them shows them anxious to get on with *A Counterblast to Agnosticism*). The family situation is exposed – a sincerely and effectively religious father, a thoroughly good practising Christian mother, a self-satisfied (but conformist) academic brother, another 'religious' brother (my inverted commas) and the rebel against dogma, Angel. Mr and Mrs Clare are presented, like the main characters we have already looked at, in the context of their time: they are good, generous-spirited, giving people, aware of social divisions but capable of rising above them in the observance of their faith. They reflect, I feel, Hardy's own generosity of spirit, something he is not freely credited with. The sons are caricatures in context. What Tess overhears, while it is in keeping with the outline we have been given of their limitations and bias, seems to show Hardy in the grip of a bias himself:

'Ah! Angel, poor Angel! I never see that nice girl [Mercy Chant] without more and more regretting his precipitancy in throwing himself away upon a dairymaid, or whatever she may be'

and from the other brother:

'He never tells me anything nowadays. His ill-considered marriage seems to have completed that estrangement from me which was begun by his extraordinary opinions . . .' (p. 376)

This completes the unchristian tone:

'Here's a pair of old boots,' he said. 'Thrown away, I suppose, by some tramp or other.'

'Some impostor who wished to come into the town barefoot, perhaps, and so excite our sympathies,' said Miss Chant. 'Yes, it must have been, for they are excellent walking-boots – by no means worn out. What a wicked thing to do! I'll carry them home for some poor person.' (p. 377)

The remarks are effective because of the personal drama of the watching Tess, but they are uncharitable, unfeeling, ungenerous, and imply the like in the speakers. Mercy Chant (note the choice of names) is *not* a 'nice girl' judging from this, and the brothers' expressions are ready-to-hand superficialities rather than felt responses. These are caricatures, and Hardy's own control of character throughout is so sustained that we tend to overlook something as stereotypic as this: there is no reason why the stereotype should not play a functional role in a realistic novel, but here we feel that Hardy has distorted for sympathetic effect.

Effective use of the stereotype is seen in the passing character of Mrs Brooks, the landlady of the lodging-house, who has to observe Tess's behaviour, half-hear her words and, above all, see the spreading stain on the ceiling. Here Hardy is writing, we feel, barely at one remove from the newspaper reporting of 'crime' or witness-box testimony which fascinated him. This reportage through character enables him ironically to direct his reader's attention to the real issues behind sensational events. But Mrs Brooks is authenticated by a natural inquisitiveness, Angel's arrival stimulating 'the feminine proclivity which had been stifled down' (p. 468) But her function is to observe, to see Tess's lips 'bleeding from the clench of her teeth' (p. 469) and finally to note her departure. By using her in this way Hardy is registering the event as it would be reported in 'every street and villa at the popular watering-place' (p. 472). In other words, the character records for the popular imagination. The deeper underlying causes, motivations, will remain unsaid. The simple character represents the simple standards and acceptances of society.

The treatment of Mr and Mrs Clare, as I have said, contrasts with this kind of presentation. If Felix and Cuthbert are shown as being superficial, Mr Clare is given a rare depth. Consider this:

... he loved his misnamed Angel, and in secret mourned over this treatment of him as Abraham might have mourned over the doomed Isaac while they went up the hill together. His silent self-generated regrets were far bitterer than the reproaches which his wife rendered audible. (p. 420)

With typical self-seriousness and complete involvement they blame themselves for what has happened – that by encouraging Angel to become a farmer they have put him in the way of 'agricultural girls' (p. 420). There is an endearing naïveté about this self-blame: the unworldliness of the Clares is their salvation and their credibility. One last glimpse of them shows them welcoming the changed Angel back from Brazil. He tells them about Tess and their response is typical of their sincerity and dedication:

... their Christianity was sure that, reprobates being their especial care, the tenderness towards Tess which her blood, her simplicity, even her poverty, had not engendered, was instantly excited by her sin. (p. 457)

This, like so many of Hardy's revisions (it was not in the *Graphic*) shows him deepening the characterization. The use of the word 'excited' is a humanizing limitation of a response to the pure woman whom they can only measure as a sinner. Their blinkered though decent attitudes and unselfish Christian practices are of their time and conditioning, but the irony which marks their presentation is compassionate, warm.

At a different place in the social scale are Dairyman Crick and his wife, again real and functional. They act as a commentary on the developing relationship between Tess and Angel, then on its development, and are silent presences at its disintegration. Crick is given substantial physical and oral presence: he even reflects on the Durbeyfield name and inheritance which is so fatal to Tess – ""'twere an old ancient race that had all but perished off the earth – though the new generations didn't know it"' (p. 162). More important are the stories he tells. The first one, about William Dewy and the praying bull, is the innocent means of interesting Tess in Angel. The second is more significant, for it is the emotional index to Tess's continuing sensitivity about her past. Before that he had indicated that Clare rejected old families – a 'caricature of Clare's opinions' (p. 184) – but Tess is of course ignorant of this and takes it to heart. The Jack Dollop story is told in Crick's inimitable manner: it contains such unconsciously pertinent phrases as 'She'll murder me!' (p. 190) and 'Not till ye make amends for ravaging her virgin innocence!' (p. 191). The stories reflect Crick's way of life in the sense that his relaxation is anecdotal, like this, the apparently harmless retailing embodying the humour and sadness of ordinary people. Mrs Crick too is important in the action. When Angel and Tess return to Talbothays after their non-honeymoon, she sounds that ominous note which is to be Tess's inward burden, that her marriage is not a marriage:

'How onnatural the brightness of her eyes did seem, and how they stood like waxen images and talked as if they were in a dream! Didn't it strike 'ee that 'twas so? Tess had always summat strange in her, and she's not now quite like the proud young bride of a well-be-doing man.' (p. 323)

The observation, the choric function – not dissimilar from that of the painter of texts, or the appearance of Groby on Christmas Eve, or the man who reports the behaviour of Marian, Izz and Retty on Tess's wedding day – all subserve the centrality of the heroine.

Throughout the narrative the passing realism of the minor characters is balanced by their functional roles in the structure. There is a constant emphasis, not surprising in view of the contained geographical area, on characters' paths crossing, of their meetings with Tess, of events and coincidences occurring which reflect character and influence the main character. The first crossing is that of Parson Tringham and Durbey-field: it sets in motion the whole train of events which culminates in the personal tragedy of Tess. Hardy's characterization is the major part of his structural coherence, a developed artistic sense of interactivity in life. It is basically realistic, but heightened by his artistic sense. No character is irrelevant in *Tess*. They all have a function and, for the most part, the presentation is authenticated by the contextual emphasis. Hardy's characters live because he knew how people lived in his context of time and place.

3. The Figurative Patterns

Hardy's presentation of character is extended by his figurative commentary on it, by the description of the backgrounds and foregrounds against which character is seen and by accumulations of both within the structure. These are simple, or subtle, or provide a varying notation of mood, situation, the influences of the past or the presentiments of the future. Take, for example, the symbolic contrast between Flintcomb-Ash (the sound, sense and associations of the words) and Talbothays (the three-syllabled spread indicating fullness) with their effect on Tess. There is an effect on a simple level too, that of seasonal contrast, and even contrast between Groby and his treatment of labour and the different treatment adopted by Dairyman Crick.

Description and figurative patterns run throughout the novel, with image and symbol woven into the structure and tightening the mesh of Tess's tragedy. Tess is associated with a number of images suggestive of innocence, of personality and of despoiling. She is part of a 'votive sisterhood' (p. 49) who take part in the club-walking, though the phrase is not in the *Graphic*. She is seen to take from nature: here, like the others, she carries 'a peeled willow wand' and 'a bunch of white flowers' (p. 50). At other times nature has given to her 'a mobile peony mouth', but just to show that she is not simply a child of nature and tradition, she has 'a red ribbon in her hair' (p. 51). I have deliberately selected from this first sequence in *Tess*, since the above phrases comprise, in their brief passing register, the whole of Tess's existence. White is innocence (her 'purity'), peony is her natural and vibrant attraction and red is blood, her own shed in violation, Prince's blood and the blood she sheds in murder. This is typical of Hardy's method in *Tess*, and we have already noted the prefigurative modes in relation to character situations. It appears simple, and sets up in the reader's mind a subliminal awareness so that such insistent patterning takes a fuller shape, corresponding perhaps to Tess's fuller and then truncated life.

When she first sees Angel she is a white shape in her 'thin white gown' (p. 55), a phrase indicative of her vulnerability. Even such detail as her greening the frock on the damp grass suggests her future fate at Alec's hands. The mixture of innocence (here unawareness), suffering (death) and blood is seen in the quick expiration of Prince, factually recorded in Tess's pallor. The solid symbol of the lodge at Trantridge being of 'crimson brick' (p. 77) is complemented by the softness of nature and the sexual innuendo when Alec feeds Tess the strawberry:

... he stood up and held it by the stem to her mouth.

'No – no!' she said quickly, putting her fingers between his hand and her lips. 'I would rather take it in my own hand.'

'Nonsense!' he insisted; and in a slight distress she parted her lips and took it in. (p. 81)

The simple act of forcing here is complemented by the later seduction: it is a preliminary in the artistic structure. Tess's basket is filled with strawberries, her person soon covered in roses, as if in natural, lush celebration of Alec's mini-triumph. And we have already noted in our study of Tess that Hardy is alerting the reader to what is going to happen by having Tess pricked by a thorn here. The figurative innuendo is complemented by the stress of the factual context: we remember that Tess is superstitious about this and thinks it the first ill-omen of the day, as perhaps many a local girl would. The strawberry is forgotten in the immediacy of the small external hurt.

Joan's *Compleat Fortune-Teller* is part of the symbolic structure, Joan's superstitions balancing Tess's and each subserving the theme of fate. The book is taken out of the house at night for fear that it will bring bad luck if left within: it is, in an innocent way, superstition given prophetic authority. Joan's use of it is reflected in her language. For instance, she refers to Tess's 'trump card' (p. 93), the fatal possession of beauty. Her husband, in his simplicity, feels that it is the d'Urberville blood. Ironically, both are right. The book and the image reach out into the novel with prefigurative force.

Tess, as I have said, is characterized by natural associations. The animal (or bird) as symbol or more commonly as pathetic image is used by Hardy as part of the unremitting focus on Tess, and there is a deliberate linking of the factual and the figurative. D'Urberville's reduction of Tib (the mare) anticipates his reduction of Tess, initially through the kiss of mastery. Just as the mare is beaten and kicks back, so Tess, her 'eyes like those of a wild animal' (p. 96) does her best to negate the forced kiss by wiping the spot on her cheek. The irony is that she cannot overcome her seduction later, though in this scene she reveals 'the red and ivory of her mouth' (p. 97), unobtrusive associations again with innocence and blood.

The Chaseborough scenes prior to the seduction are heavy with fate, like Tess setting off late to Trantridge and, above all, her interaction, as we have seen, with Alec's mistresses. Both are 'trump cards', as Hardy makes clear in a finely low-key association which looks forward to Tess's fate: 'a dark virago, Car Darch, dubbed Queen of Spades, till lately a favourite of d'Urberville's; Nancy, her sister, nick-named the Queen of Diamonds; and the young married woman who had already tumbled down' (p. 110). It is a kind of figurative sick joke, and one is inclined to say that the cards are stacked against Tess – the unmarried woman is about to tumble down too. Much later in the action the two Queens reappear at Flintcomb-Ash, and here Hardy's subtly reticent focus achieves a marked tension. Tess recognizes them but they don't recognize her.

We have already glanced at the painter of texts in his functional role, but it is worth noticing the red paint, the damnations recorded in it and their oblique references (at least in her mind) to Tess. They are reminder and warning: letters of fiery red seem to broadcast her guilt. Here Tess is returning home, but Hardy uses travelling fact and journeying metaphor as commentary on Tess's state and, more particularly, the incidence of her death-wish. She is put into the stone coffin by Angel when he sleepwalks (Chapter XXXVII) and after the 'house-ridding' she sleeps over the d'Urberville vault (Chapter LII). The links between real and metaphorical journeys and death are established after Tess comes home: here she is on the first Monday contemplating her future – 'she saw before her a long and stony highway which she had to tread, without aid, and with little sympathy. Her depression was then terrible, and she could have hidden herself in a tomb' (p. 133). This simple language (Tess's consciousness is for the most part explicit) is an understated formula for structured art. The text of the novel is filled with such seemingly casual pronouncements, but we should notice here how easily they are set in the personal, factual, traditional context. Factual and figurative complement each other in the narrative coherence.

Tess's travels of the imagination (so often retrospective) are more than balanced by the physical journeys she takes. She wanders at night in her loneliness when she first comes home, and sees herself as 'a figure of Guilt intruding into the haunts of Innocence' (p. 135). The simple personification indicates Tess's nature, but again there is a carrying forward in the structure. A later night-wandering finds her settled in the wood, disturbed until dawn by the noises. She strangles the wounded birds 'tenderly', thus dispatching injured innocence, where the guilt belongs to others, but of course the tenuous imaginative innuendo links this to the killing of Alec later and the finality of judicial guilt which follows. Hardy can be both explicit and associative in his use of fact and figure.

A particularized use of symbol is seen in Hardy's account of the reaping machine and its effects. Here it is in action:

The narrow lane of stubble encompassing the field grew wider with each circuit, and the standing corn was reduced to a smaller area as the morning wore on. Rabbits, hares, snakes, mice, retreated inwards as into a fastness, unaware of the ephemeral nature of their refuge, and of the doom that awaited them later in the day when, their covert shrinking to a more and more horrible narrowness, they were huddled together, friends and foes, till the last few yards of upright wheat fell also under the teeth of the unerring reaper, and they were every one put to death by the sticks and stones of the harvesters. (p. 137)

The anticipatory force of this and its centrality in the structure of the novel is evident. The cumulative effect of certain words and phrases has unequivocal associations – *retreated, unaware, . . . of the doom, the unerring reaper, put to death*. The mechanistic president of the mortals has finished his sport. Man's treatment of innocent nature is equated with his treatment of humanity. The machine is as inexorable as fate. Tess's child, and later Tess, will fall to the 'unerring reaper'.

For Tess there is no retreat. The field-women working with her sing ballads which are traditional but which point across at this local example of seduction: later Tess herself seeks out Angel's favourite ballads and sings them as the small comfort of his absence. The sad irony attending both sequences is in the muted happiness she feels in the company of her workmates, a happiness fated to be transitory. The immediate tragedy (of Sorrow) comes quickly upon her, and once more the unobtrusive descriptions provide a running association with what has gone and what is to come. Not only has Tess 'a thick cable of twisted dark hair' (p. 144) – looking back to Car Darch's treacle and obliquely forward to her own hanging – but she has 'a red spot' in the middle of each cheek, while the reflection of the candle in her eyes makes them shine 'like a diamond' (p. 145). Both references look back and forward with a sharp resonance. The diamond comparison reminds us of Joan's metaphor of the baby's eyes (here we are witnessing the death of what Hardy expressively calls 'a child's child' (p. 144): it anticipates by association the real diamonds, the family gift which Tess wears on her wedding evening – 'She bent forward, at which each diamond on her neck gave a sinister wink like a toad's' (p. 293). Once again the casually figurative and the real are connected.

Another significant emphasis occurs when Angel first hears Tess's voice and her talk about ghosts. Crick is so absorbed by what she is saying that he plants his knife and fork 'erect on the table, like the beginning of a gallows' (p. 175). This, at the very beginning of Tess's relationship with Angel, which is ultimately to lead to her execution, is an ominous image, but there is always method in Hardy's figurative choices. We need not strain at it or overload it with too much weight: it almost connects in its artistry with the superstitions of the heroine.

This is followed by a heavily symbolic garden scene which compresses many of the elements of Hardy's figurative usage. The scene has often been analysed by critics – it is sufficiently outstanding to merit close attention – but it is worth looking at it here because of its facts and figures combination, in which observation and imaginative treatment cohere. I give the preceding paragraph, which is essential to a full understanding of its impact:

Tess had heard those notes in the attic above her head. Dim, flattened, constrained by their confinement, they had never appealed to her as now, when they wandered in the still air with a stark quality like that of nudity. To speak absolutely, both instrument and execution were poor; but the relative is all, and as she listened Tess, like a fascinated bird, could not leave the spot. Far from leaving she drew up towards the performer, keeping behind the hedge that he might not guess her presence.

The outskirt of the garden in which Tess found herself had been left uncultivated for some years, and was now damp and rank with juicy grass which sent up mists of pollen at a touch; and with tall blooming weeds emitting offensive smells – weeds whose red and yellow and purple hues formed a polychrome as dazzling as that of cultivated flowers. She went stealthily as a cat through this profusion of growth, gathering cuckoo-spittle on her skirts, cracking snails that were underfoot, staining her hands with thistle-milk and slug-slime, and rubbing off upon her naked arms sticky blights which, though snow-white on the apple-tree trunks, made madder stains on her skin; thus she drew quite near to Clare, still unobserved of him. (pp. 178–9)

There is an excellent analysis of this and the paragraphs which surround it in James Gibson's 'Master Guide' to *Tess of the d'Urbervilles* (pp. 69–72). Two simple comparisons, of Tess with bird and cat, show Hardy's subtlety here. One reflects her vulnerability, the other her latent sexuality, and both are repeated in the novel as indicators of those and related qualities. What is of central interest is that cats kill birds, that Tess's unconscious sexuality makes her more vulnerable, that her sensitivity is innocently killed. The images represent the conflict within her too. And it is interesting here to see Hardy's first thoughts (or revisionary afterthoughts): 'madder' was originally 'blood red' in the *Graphic* version, where Tess was merely brushing off snails rather than crushing them. The innocence–violence motif ('madder' produces red dye) is still here, but more particularly the 'pure' Tess injures innocent nature, just as she has been injured herself. The overall effect is one of contamination. And thus, in her movement towards Clare, a mini-journey in itself, the garden is symbolic of what has happened in her life. Tess is the victim who is injured and stained, and who injures and stains others – at the very least in her own mind. This scene, like so much in the novel, is infused with her past and prophetic of her future. In this present she is moving towards the future, the accumulations of the garden marking her progress. The factual and symbolic interlock: every detail in the scene can carry the weight of imaginative interpretation because of Hardy's consummate perspective.

With the entry of Clare into her life Hardy employs colours with rather a different emphasis. Here is Angel's view of Tess, and we might compare it with Alec's practice:

He had never before seen a woman's lips and teeth which forced upon his mind with such persistent iteration the old Elizabethan simile of roses filled with snow. (p. 209)

I have referred to this elsewhere (see p. 49) in relation to Clare's character, but here the quotation from Campion ('like rose-buds filled with snow') not only provides Clare with the literary analogy but Hardy with an ironic opportunity to develop the colour motif in a different way. We are reminded of Tess and the roses and thorns, but at the same time her appearance belies any hint of past suffering. The perfection Clare sees is part of her tragedy, but no literary analogy can distance her from experience.

As Angel moves from literary abstraction to life Hardy personifies place – as he often does – in this instance to convey Angel's romanticism:

The aged and lichened brick gables breathed forth 'Stay!' The windows smiled, the door coaxed and beckoned, the creeper blushed confederacy. A personality within it was so far-reaching in her influence as to spread and make the bricks, mortar, and whole overhanging sky throb with a burning sensibility. (p. 214)

The place is the dairy-house: it becomes reflective of character mood which spreads throughout the small milking community both as idyll and idyll invested with irony. The atmosphere is personalized in Tess and Angel. The suggestive nature of the imagery carries the deepening sexual awareness, but it is also dangerous and subtly prefigurative on occasions. When Clare returns from his visit to his parents he sees Tess shortly after she has woken up in the afternoon: Hardy describes 'the red interior of her mouth as if it had been a snake's' (p. 231), the comparison implying that she could strike him, as indeed she does, though of course the wound is mental and emotional. Since our sympathies are generally with Tess, the image is sudden, unexpected, as quick and striking as her wedding-night revelations. Her fascination, her sexuality, is conveyed in another image – she is 'warm as a sunned cat' (p. 232). Even here we are aware of the latent power: she looks at Angel 'as Eve at her second waking might have regarded Adam' (p. 232). The snake image is still in our minds, but the Biblical analogies which run throughout the novel are an ironic commentary on situation as well as being critical (or cynical) of Christian practice. The garden scene referred to above may have been paradisaical but it was also of the earth earthy. Here the images of Tess convey her personality and give her situation a universality throughout time.

The imagery from nature continues expressive. When she feels Angel's love we are told that 'she seemed to flinch under it like a plant in too burning a sun' (p. 232). This shows her vulnerability in terms of the nature to which she is so close at times. Such images establish her as she is and as she appears, and since much of the novel is concerned with what appears as distinct from what actually is, this figurative practice is an underlining. Reinforcing her vulnerability through natural analogy is Hardy's suspenseful narrative, and the story within a story reappears at this juncture. Her palpitating love for Angel is again undercut by Jack Dollop: Mrs Crick's comment on the ghost of the first husband troubling the second – and the need for complete honesty about the past – can only wound the silent Tess. Here Hardy's deft placing of the story in his structure ensures the maximum effect on Tess, for Tess is at the time struggling to combat her own jealousy over the other girls. Tess, choking over her food, is forced to contribute to the morality of the story in general agreement with her companions. The story exemplifies, symbolizes her own case: the fact of her past exacerbates her suffering. She thinks in terms of religious analogy: 'Yes, there was the pain of it. This question of a woman telling her story – the heaviest of crosses to herself – seemed but amusement to others. It was as if people should laugh at martyrdom' (p. 244). The last phrase was not in the *Graphic*: it heightens our recognition of Tess's suffering.

When Angel and Tess drive with the milk to the station (he draws her attention to the d'Urberville manor-house) she is described as having 'the suspended attitude of a friendly leopard at pause' (p. 251). The latent power – and danger – seen earlier are emphasized here, and the danger is given an inverted twist in relation to her past with the idea of her treading on it as 'one treads on a coal that is smouldering' (p. 257).

The simple image suggests the dangerous game that Tess is playing, and it is at this stage that Clare learns of her d'Urberville antecedents, suggests that she spells her name in that way in the future and spells out himself the fact that her family name will smooth the way with his parents. In doing so he uses Joan's image: ' "My dear girl – a d'Urberville hurt the dignity of a Clare! It is a grand card to play – that of you belonging to such a family" ' (p. 259). Hardy's considered use of figurative echo is part of the novel's fatalistic pattern.

When Tess joins her companions shortly afterwards they are 'like a row of avenging ghosts' (p. 263) and they hang 'about her in their white nightgowns' (p. 264). Both these references look backwards and forwards in the narrative. Before the wedding Angel buys Tess a gown, and immediately her mother's ballad comes into her mind. Hardy prints only two lines of this in the book version of his novel, but in the *Graphic* he makes the connection with Tess's past much more clearly. Her fear that the dress would change colour is symptomatic of the rooted insecurity which she feels; in the omitted stanzas red, green and black are mentioned, with their obvious connotations of red for blood, green for innocence and black for death. Hardy's cuts reflect his artistic sensibility, a judgement against over-writing motifs at this stage. We are near the revelation, which is the climax of the sequence and must speak for itself without too much figurative obtrusion. But the inter-active echoes are there: while the letter goes under the carpet and delays Tess's confession, Angel is thinking of his family and 'the grand card with which he meant to surprise them ere long' (p. 276). The marriage over, there is the inept account of the d'Urberville coach and the afternoon crow of the cock – 'the white one with the rose comb' (p. 282). If nature is ominous, so is art, and the farmhouse which was once a d'Urberville mansion has factual and figurative significance. Although it is somewhat stagey and is, after all, a whim of Clare's inverted snobbery, the resemblance of the portraits to Tess registers a decadent inheritance. The physical distortions symbolize the distortions within her own mind, an index to her thoughts of herself given visual immediacy. Phrases like 'suggestive of merciless treachery' (p. 283), while they can have no application to Tess, call up her own capacity for self-blame and anticipate Clare's reception of what she has done. Even in the pleasantries and mingling of hands which follow, the sun appears to single out Tess, its beam through the small opening making 'a spot like a paint-mark set upon her' (p. 284). Inevitably we are reminded of the stain upon her in her own eyes, in the eyes of conventional judge-ment, and we recall the texts of the painter and Tess's seeing her own guilt in them. When the sun has gone there comes from nature another insistent reminder of the past – 'the restful dead leaves of the preceding autumn were stirred to irritated resurrection' (p. 285). Tess, ever consonant with nature and its moods, is stirred by Angel's confidence to unirritated resurrection of her past, but before this happens she 'winced like a wounded animal' (p. 285) when Angel accuses her of not being cheerful. It seems that Hardy is bringing together at this climactic moment, the verbal echoes which are associated with Tess's fate. The diamonds arrive, there is an innocent reminder of the cock crowing that afternoon, Angel confesses, Tess follows. There is 'a Last Day luridness in this red-coaled glow' while 'A large shadow of her shape rose upon the wall and ceiling' (pp. 292–3). Judgement, the fire of the past not stamped out, the shadow: the descriptive power registers the terrible finality.

There is no let-up now in the figurative treatment of the crisis: 'Clare arose in the light of a dawn that was ashy and furtive, as though associated with crime' (p. 306), and we note how cunningly Hardy has entered Clare's mood and consciousness through the figurative language which defines his state. Hardy does not let go of Angel's consciousness for long at this stage, or of Tess's either, but whereas Tess's reactions are predictable (they arise from the deep-rooted fears becoming irrevocable fact) Angel's are probed at subconscious level. The dream sequence is one of the most powerfully poignant episodes in the novel. Angel's dream contains his memories and his wishes, and the sleepwalking symbolizes the nature of his reactions to the experiences he has just undergone with Tess. His taking her in his arms reflects a love and tenderness which, as Tess ruefully notes, he cannot display in their waking lives. His placing her in the stone coffin is his submerged death-wish for her, ironically complementing her often expressed death-wish for herself. In the structure of the narrative it anticipates her lying on the sacrificial block at Stonehenge. The symbolism and the reality are as one. The passage, like the garden sequence, repays close attention, since in addition to its central relevance it has literary echoes (notably of Lear and Cordelia) and the might-have-been which is a constant in Hardy's art. The dream symbolizes the divisions within Angel (and also I think the divisions within Tess). He might have woken up, she might have told him the next day: the alternatives become a symbolic presence in the novel. And since they are *not* translated into fact, they remain an unvoiced figurative commentary on what did happen.

Image and symbol accumulate as Tess's adversity deepens. Her compassionate strangling of the birds anticipates her killing of Alec and her own death – she and the birds are linked of course as victims of human nature and nature. The birds are reality which complement the image so often used of the vulnerable heroine. At Flintcomb-Ash the winter is severe, and everything conduces to Tess's suffering. Here Hardy uses image and symbol in contradistinction, the first from the sophistications of a game, the second from nature. Winter 'came on in stealthy and measured glides, like the moves of a chess-player' (p. 363), the image suggesting one of the many accumulations of Fate. Of greater interest is the omniscient introduction of the 'nameless' birds who arrive at Flintcomb-Ash – 'gaunt spectral creatures with tragical eyes – eyes which had witnessed scenes of cataclysmal horror in inaccessible polar regions' (p. 363). The effect of the descriptive touches is to draw the birds into direct association with Tess, 'tragical' and 'horror' being descriptive of her appearance and suffering. There is an additional suggestion too: they are seeking their own place where they would be at one with nature. Their journey, like Tess's journeys, provides only temporary respite. Their element, like Talbothays, has gone.

Other descriptions are anticipatory, as often in Hardy. For instance, the warm-walled cottage has a roof which 'had turned itself into a gymnasium of all the winds' (p. 364). This is verbally, descriptively close to Tess's experience at Stonehenge, where her fate is sealed, the connected images showing the fragility of existence. We recall (see p. 40) that her journey to see the Clares is dogged by the symbol of the 'Cross-in-Hand, where the stone pillar stands desolate and silent, to mark the site of a miracle, a murder, or both' (p. 373). I quote this again for the symbolic resonances. Tess carries her own cross with her – it is always in hand – while 'desolate', 'miracle' and 'murder' represent her situation, her present hope and the reality to come. The irony plays over her visit: the miracle was to hand had she but known it, for the Clares would have given her physical and emotional sustenance. And the might-have-been here is oppressively within reach.

She encounters a miracle almost immediately after the visit in the person of the converted Alec d'Urberville. He accompanies her as far as the Cross-in-Hand, thus giving the symbol a further twist, while Hardy deepens the commentary with some account of the legends associated with it and stresses the 'sinister' and 'solemn' nature of the relic (p. 389). The relic becomes central to the interaction between Tess and Alec, who says to her, '"put your hand upon that stone hand, and swear that you will never tempt me – by your charms or ways"' (p. 390). The convert is unwillingly admitting to superstition, but this ominous moment is extended when Tess asks a shepherd '"the meaning of that old stone I have passed"'' (p. 391). The story of the malefactor who 'sold his soul to the devil' (p. 391) upsets Tess. It is a simple, significant, if somewhat Gothic symbol of what she considers to be her sin.

With Alec's return colour returns too. He is first seen as a black speck on the skyline, then as 'a man in black' (p. 392), his clerical garb at a distance taking on the appearance of death. If Alec is death to Tess, a greater symbol conjures death too. Here is the threshing-machine and the engine which powers it and its attendant:

A little way off there was another indistinct figure; this one black, with a sustained hiss that spoke of strength very much in reserve. The long chimney running up beside an ash-tree, and the warmth which radiated from the spot, explained without the necessity of much daylight that here was the engine which was to act as the *primum mobile* of this little world. By the engine stood a dark motionless being, a sooty and grimy embodiment of tallness, in a sort of trance, with a heap of coals by his side: it was the engine-man. The isolation of his manner and colour lent him the appearance of a creature from Tophet, who had strayed into the pellucid smokelessness of this region of yellow grain and pale soil, with which he had nothing in common, to amaze and discompose its aborigines. (pp. 404–5)

He has no interest in his surroundings, and is intent only on his engine. The associations are immediate. The intruder-outsider who reduces nature, interferes with natural life, approximates to the outsiders who reduce Tess's life, Alec d'Urberville and, and this is ironic, Angel Clare. Each interferes with her nature, Alec with his initially mechanistic seductive sexuality, Angel with his mechanistic theories. The red and black motif – fire and death – is here invoked with a somewhat different emphasis. There are Biblical associations, suggestions of hell on earth, the particularity of the description underlying Hardy's own resentment and bias. The simple way of life has changed: Tess and the field-workers are slaves to the machine, victims of its power. It is noteworthy that in the previous paragraph Hardy refers to the machine as 'the red tyrant' (p. 404). It is obviously part of the structural coherence of the novel that at two critical junctures the machines which dictate work should be seen against the life of the heroine: the reaping and the threshing are natural equivalents to her state at the time. In each case the machine provides the commentary on and the contrast with palpitating human nature.

Tess's own red tyrant (though dressed in black) is Alec d'Urberville, and she draws prefigurative blood when she strikes him with her gauntlet – 'A scarlet oozing appeared . . . and in a moment the blood began dropping from his mouth upon the straw' (p. 411). Immediately

74

after this, as if to emphasize that she is his natural victim, Tess looks at him 'with the hopeless defiance of the sparrow's gaze before its captor twists its neck'. She also cries out, '"Once victim, always victim – that's the law!"' (p. 411).

We have already glanced briefly at Tess's attempts to perfect the ballads that Angel loved. It is part of her dream (and we know she is often in a reverie), with the songs taking the place of the longed-for reality and supplying the happy memories of what once was. But with her return home because of her mother's illness, the hell and fire associations are picked up in the allotment sequence when Alec appears, his face being lit up by the fire. He is quite alive to his symbolic role, even quoting *Paradise Lost*, a cunning structural link on Hardy's part with that mixed paradisaical garden where Tess walked, listening to Angel's music. Alec says, '"A jester might say that this is just like Paradise. You are Eve and I am the old Other One come to tempt you in the disguise of an inferior animal"' (p. 431). This is superbly done, for we have the impression that the sardonic jester – President of his fictional immortals – is Hardy himself playing a dark joke through Biblical analogy as commentary on the hounding of his heroine. That hounding continues to the very end with the death of Sir John, the persistence of Alec and, above all, the weighted fact and symbol of the d'Urberville vault where the family spends the night. The associations here go right back to the beginning of the novel, with the news of the family and the few meagre relics which this impoverished branch possesses. The linking is done visually and naturally: there is the description of 'a beautifully traceried window, of many lights, its date being the fifteenth century. It was called the d'Urberville window, and in the upper part could be discerned heraldic emblems like those on Durbeyfield's old seal and spoon' (p. 447). The associations of the vault exacerbate Tess's death-wish, and she exclaims bitterly at still being alive. Meanwhile the pulse of Hardy's imagery beats strongly: in the letter which Marian and Izz send to Angel we find '"A woman should not be try'd beyond her strength, and continual dropping will wear away a Stone – ay, more – a Diamond"' (p. 450). The simple language reflects the simple sincere values, but stones – from Cross-in-Hand to Stonehenge – show the simple hardness of Tess's lot, while the diamond associations have already been indicated. When Angel returns and goes to Marlott he sees the inscription of the headstone 'John Durbeyfield, rightly d'Urberville' with 'HOW ARE THE MIGHTY FALLEN'. This picks up Tringham's quotation of the phrase (from II Samuel i, 19, 25) in the first chapter, and shows how carefully Hardy is tracing the various milestones which mark Tess's journey from life to death.

75

From now on Hardy brings together in his climactic sequence all those associations which have been actively producing the artistic effects of figurative patterning. When Angel and Tess are brought together 'She seemed to feel like a fugitive in a dream' and 'her hands, which, once rosy, were now white and more delicate' (p. 466). We note the implication of diminished innocence. With the murder Mrs Brooks first sees a spot, notices that it is red and then that the 'oblong white ceiling, with this scarlet blot in the midst, had the appearance of a gigantic ace of hearts' (p. 471). In the movement of impetuous passion Tess is linked to the card image again with conclusive irony: Hardy inserted this image in the book version (it was not in the *Graphic*), his structural awareness once more in evidence. He is, as I said, bringing it all together, sounding the notes already used as accompaniment to the action with explicit resonance.

Tess follows Clare after this and, just as at the beginning of the novel she had been a white figure watching him, so now he sees 'a moving spot intruded on the white vacuity of its [the road's] perspective' (p. 473). She has, when she speaks, a 'pitiful white smile' (p. 474). When she reports the fact that she has killed Alec she is 'in a reverie' (p. 474). The deserted mansion is seen as contrast to the d'Urberville one of their honeymoon or the fake d'Urberville's dwelling at Trantridge. Stonehenge is a 'very Temple of the Winds' (p. 484), which produce 'a booming tone, like the note of some gigantic one-stringed harp' (p. 483). The patterning, the echoes, are too obvious to need comment.

From Cross-in-Hand to Stonehenge is the final 'Phase' in Tess's journey. The last description is telling in its factual and figurative force:

He went to the stone, and bent over her, holding one poor little hand; her breathing now was quick and small, like that of a lesser creature than a woman. All waited in the growing light, their faces and hands as if they were silvered, the remainder of their figures dark, the stones glistening green-gray, the Plain still a mass of shade. Soon the light was strong, and a ray shone upon her unconscious form, peering under her eyelids and waking her. (p. 487)

The colours are finely handled, the light, the dark, the animal association here with sublime pathos which characterizes Tess, the stone itself: it is almost as if the red of the life-force (and violence) has gone from her. The final fact and figure is the black flag of execution. The factual and the figurative, blended throughout the novel and sometimes merging with imaginative certitude, come to the irrevocable 'Fulfilment' of the artistic and human ending.

4. Dialect and Dialogue: The Means of Authenticity

One of Hardy's major strengths as a writer of novels and stories is his ability to define and differentiate character through speech. We have already seen how Tess is known inwardly and outwardly, how commentary and the spoken word coalesce to produce the verisimilitude of character in action. This speech is often the natural expression of thought, emotion, reflecting the demands of the moment or, as in this instance from Alec, its opportunities concealed by consideration.

'Nights grow chilly in September. Let me see.' He pulled off a lightweight coat that he had worn, and put it round her tenderly. 'That's it – now you'll feel warmer,' he continued. 'Now, my pretty, rest there; I shall soon be back again.' (p. 118)

This is mood speech in character, not literary (note the repetition of 'now', the directness, the tone): apart from uttering her name on his return, these are the last words that Alec speaks before the seduction. And though Hardy gives Alec many voices – that of melodramatic and stagey stereotype and fervent preacher – the registers accurately reflect the roles he plays. Hardy knows that in life individuals project images of themselves verbally as well as visually, and Alec is an actor as the occasion presents itself – here with Tess tenderness may serve the immediate purpose. By presenting his moods through his language Hardy is identifying very closely with his creature, for Alec is essentially the slave to passion and simulated passion. His verbal opportunism is a character trait, his movements and shifts a linguistic equivalent of his false name. Just as he has acquired an identity so he plays up to it in words – squire, preacher, protector.

Angel is what he is largely through Hardy's evaluative commentary, though his words again underline particular character and personality traits. In adversity with Tess he achieves a fuller utterance though it is often marred by an incipient pedantry, as with the inappropriate use of 'prestidigitation'. His speech is an index, for he lives more in analogy than reality. Here he is speaking to Tess before he 'confesses':

'Put your head there, because I want you to forgive me and not to be indignant with me for not telling you before, as perhaps I ought to have done . . . I did not mention it because I was afraid of endangering my chance of you, darling, the great prize of my life – my Fellowship I call you. My brother's Fellowship was won at his college, mine at Talbothays Dairy.' (p. 291)

Apart from the rich authorial irony playing over this (can we *really* believe that Angel believes he might have lost Tess, who is always subservient, almost deferential to him?), there is condescension and possession, the analogy a figure rather than a felt emotion. It is a man conscious of his education and of his change of direction, but defensive about that change of direction to such an extent that he has to refer to it. It is as if he has moved in the flesh but not in the spirit: it reflects his incapacity for life until it is 'too late'.

Tess herself has the two registers which Hardy defines, yet there is, I think, some weakness in her verbal presentation. Here is Tess early in the novel at home:

'I'll rock the cradle for 'ee, mother,' said the daughter gently. 'Or I'll take off my best frock and help you wring up? I thought you had finished long ago ... Had it anything to do with father's making such a mommet of himself in thik carriage this afternoon? Why did 'er! I felt inclined to sink into the ground with shame!' (p. 58)

This seems to teeter uneasily between the heroine who is of the poor and speaks as they do, and the heroine who is idealized by her creator and is just about to emerge from the family cocoon. And here is Tess in angry bitterness, speaking directly and convincingly – ' "My God! I could knock you out of the gig! Did it never strike your mind that what every woman says some women may feel?" ' (p. 125) The last part of this last sentence has been revised (it was originally the feeble 'a woman might smile innocently') and we note that this is in the other register. Again we are aware of Hardy's strong identification with her: the language is from the heart, for she is already a victim – and its forthrightness is typical of Tess at this stage in her development.

At one stage Tess recites (I choose the word deliberately) the experiences which contribute to her own mystical individuality:

'I don't know about ghosts,' she was saying; 'but I do know that our souls can be made to go outside our bodies when we are alive ... A very easy way to feel 'em go ... is to lie on the grass at night and look straight up at some big bright star; and, by fixing your mind upon it, you will soon find that you are hundreds and hundreds o' miles away from your body, which you don't seem to want at all.' (p. 175)

One feels that the "em" and the "o" are makeweights in the natural flow of this imaginative girl, who is generally shy and apprehensive. Tess's speech does not need Angel's tutelage, and in her crisis with Angel dialect and colloquial abbreviations are eliminated in the interest of direct and moving statement, though there are the natural solecisms of stress:

'I thought, Angel, that you loved me – me, my very self! If it is I you do love, O how can it be that you look and speak so? It frightens me! Having begun to love you, I love you for ever – in all changes, in all disgraces, because you are yourself. I ask no more. Then how can you, O my own husband, stop loving me?' (pp. 298–9)

The sentiments show the quality of Tess's character, some of their expressions the quality of Hardy's idealization, where the grammatical and exclamatory perhaps outweigh spontaneity. We see her later, in a rather different emotional extremity, recurring to her natural and unforced idiom when she strangles the birds.

When she is at Flintcomb-Ash Tess is more described than verbalized by Hardy. Her speech forms a deliberate contrast, I feel, with her factual image as field-woman and her inward image, treasured and poignant, of being Mrs Angel Clare. This is how she speaks to Marian after the latter has told her of Angel's proposal to Izz Huett:

'No. It is a very good thing that you have done. I have been living on in a thirtover, lackaday way, and have not seen where it may lead to! I ought to have sent him a letter oftener. He said I could not go to him, but he didn't say I was not to write as often as I liked. I won't dally like this any longer! I have been very wrong and neglectful in leaving everything to be done by him!' (p. 370)

Apart from the subjective intensity of this, it is interesting to note that the two registers have been combined – 'thirtover' the natural local expression, but the rest the simple and self-blaming mode we have come to expect.

Tess's speech hardly survives Hardy's identification at times. Here she is again during the brief idyll with Angel:

'I fear that what you think of me now may not last. I do not wish to outlive your present feeling for me. I would rather not. I would rather be dead and buried when the time comes for you to despise me, so that it may never be known to me that you despised me.' (p. 481)

Even the natural repetition cannot save this or inject the genuine note of reality. But the remarkable thing is that despite the authorial possessiveness, idealization and identification which characterize the presentation of Tess, Hardy's genius is such that the character transcends much of her utterance. And moreover, since she is between two social worlds in spirit, in feeling, in sympathetic affiliations, Tess's language sometimes naturally possesses the hybrid qualities of her conditioning. The midnight baptism feels and reads right despite the omniscient gloss where Hardy mentions 'the stopt-diapason note which her voice acquired when her heart was in her speech, *and which will never be forgotten by those who knew her*' (p. 145, my italics). When she speaks, the real and the ideal coalesce at best. Hardy's emotional integration with her was such that he wrote her poem 'Tess's Lament' (published in *Poems of the Past and the Present*, 1902) from her own supposed inwardness. Occasional abbreviations give hints of rustic speech, and the death-wish runs right through the poem. The second verse in some ways approximates to the balanced utterance of Tess's outward speech in the novel:

> 'Ah! dairy where I lived so long,
>> I lived so long,
> Where I would rise up staunch and strong,
>> And lie down hopefully.
> 'Twas there within the chimney-seat
> He watched me to the clock's slow beat –
> Loved me, and learnt to call me Sweet,
>> And whispered words to me.

For Hardy, the identification lasted, one feels, for the rest of his life.

Other characters whose speech is received standard English are Mr and Mrs Clare and the other sons, though the last two might well have affectations which Hardy leaves unrecorded. But it is with the range of rural characters that Hardy achieves an unqualified authenticity. We have already heard some of these characters; Joan is particularly fluent in response to the good news:

'That were all a part of the larry. We've been found to be the greatest gentlefolk in the whole county – reaching all back long before Oliver Grumble's time – to the days of the Pagan Turks – with monuments, and vaults, and crests, and 'scutcheons, and the Lord knows what all. In Saint Charles's days we was made Knights o' the Royal Oak, our real name being d'Urberville! ... Don't that make your bosom plim? 'Twas on this account that your father rode home in the vlee; not because he'd been drinking, as people supposed.' (pp. 58–9)

The zest, the errors, the excitement, the lie, all these show Hardy recording the natural speech of his character with uncondescending delight. There is a vivacity and verve about Joan's language which engages us. Joan is of her time, but her thought processes and the words which emerge are of all time.

So strong is the impress of individuality through speech that we feel the closeness of Hardy's observation of oral tradition and practice. 'Sir John', the children, Marian, for instance, all have the vivid verbal stamp. Tess's father is moved to rash decision by the accretion of new-found pride:

'No,' said he stoically, 'I won't sell his old body. When we d'Urbervilles was knights in the land, we didn't sell our chargers for cat's meat. Let 'em keep their shillings! He've served me well in his lifetime, and I won't part from him now.' (p. 75)

Here there is little dialect but the language perfectly conveys the nature of this wayward, shiftless, impulsive and wrong-headed man. Hardy's mastery of dialect in the novel is such that, like George Eliot before him, he uses it with something approaching artistic reticence. It must not obscure meaning, but it must reflect character, locality, tradition. Hardy's rural characters in *Tess* rarely rise to the fluent proverbialisms of Mrs Poyser in *Adam Bede*, for their language reflects the economic and social circumstances of their inheritance.

The exchanges at Talbothays involving the various helpers and dairy-maids have Hardy's seal of authenticity. The stories about Jack Dollop which so wound Tess cause Beck Knibbs to observe

'All's fair in love and war. I'd ha' married en just as she did, and if he'd said two words to me about not telling him anything whatsomdever about my first chap that I hadn't chose to tell, I'd ha' knocked him down wi' the rolling-pin – a scram little feller like he!' (p. 244)

The trouble is that one particular woman couldn't, and she is listening to what is said. Here the earthy speech, the aggressive physicality lacking in Tess, serve as a deliberate contrast with her. Beck's words stress the struggles and conflicts of life, the war of the sexes within marriage, without recourse to morality or conscience. Hardy is here using common speech to define a common situation. It is also obliquely Tess's situation, and if she were of the same type as Beck she would be easily absorbed into knockabout life. Here Hardy's irony is built into the rural language. Tess is aware of Angel as well as of her own past, and he is far from being a 'scram [puny, weak] little feller'.

On her return from her frustrating visit to the Clares, Tess meets an old woman. The reality of the language is used to disturb Tess's consciousness, though this time she has no foreboding. She asks if everyone has gone to church in the village of Evershead:

'No, my dear,' said the old woman. "Tis too soon for that; the bells hain't strook out yet. They be all gone to hear the preaching in yonder barn. A ranter preaches there between the services – an excellent, fiery, Christian man they say. But, Lord, I don't go to hear'n! What comes in the regular way over the pulpit is hot enough for I.' (p. 379)

Here the naturalness of the speech and the irony it contains are important. It is descriptive of the as yet unrevealed Alec d'Urberville – 'ranter' is good, 'fiery, Christian' aptly ironic. But the real focus, which stresses Tess as victim, is surely seen in the fact that she is virtually directed towards impassioned Christianity, having just come from what she feels is unchristian rejection. And the old woman's words, simple, spoken from her local context, represent the natural, ignorant appraisal that passes for truth. Tess is to discover the truth for herself almost immediately.

The speech of Hardy's rural characters is sometimes chorus commentary on events, particularly those affecting the heroine. Sometimes they are merely witnesses to her situations, but their words are generally charged with significance within the artistic structure of the novel. They have the natural colloquial and dialect usages of their place and time, and their realism makes the texture of *Tess* at once satisfying and complete. Their speech is the major part of their individual and local reality.

5. The Omniscient Author

Hardy, like the great Victorian novelists before him, employs a number of omniscient modes, some of which have been glanced at earlier in this study. They rarely impede the narrative flow, and often they act as commentary on that narrative as it is proceeding. For example, the seduction of Tess is accompanied by perspective philosophical commentary:

Why it was that upon this beautiful feminine tissue, sensitive as gossamer, and practically blank as snow as yet, there should have been traced such a coarse pattern as it was doomed to receive; why so often the coarse appropriates the finer thus, the wrong man the woman, the wrong woman the man, many thousand years of analytical philosophy have failed to explain to our sense of order. One may, indeed, admit the possibility of a retribution lurking in the present catastrophe. Doubtless some of Tess d'Urberville's mailed ancestors rollicking home from a fray had dealt the same measure even more ruthlessly towards peasant girls of their time. But though to visit the sins of the fathers upon the children may be a morality good enough for divinities, it is scorned by average human nature; and it therefore does not mend the matter. (p. 119)

Putting aside the possibly autobiographical note of 'the wrong man the woman', the impressive thing about this authorial comment is the amount of associative reference that Hardy gets into this paragraph. Tess's vulnerability is doubly conveyed by the fragility of the gossamer analogy and the use of 'blank' in the snow one. The emphasis on humanity in interaction as distinct from theories (philosophy) about it sounds one of the themes of the novel. The 'retribution' shows Hardy forecasting with casual, even unobtrusive statement the ironic denouement of his own novel. The reference to Tess as a d'Urberville – even when she knows she is one she asserts her preference to be called Durbeyfield – is an imaginative condensing of her inheritance, her present and her future. She *does* become a d'Urberville, through the resemblance to the portraits in the honeymoon farmhouse, through Angel's pride in her family, through her night by the d'Urberville vault, and finally and most ironically, as mistress to the fake d'Urberville. The reference to the 'mailed ancestors' looks back (and forward to the vault) but it also links Tess immediately to the 'peasant girls of their time'. The mention of Exodus is part of Hardy's Biblical notation which runs the length of the novel, with here a bitter irony which comes across despite the clichéd end of the sentence which, in a way, reflects 'average human nature' in the language of its comprehension.

This is a full authorial commentary at the crisis point of the novel, the end of the 'Phase' of innocence. Though Hardy is thought to be outspoken – and he often is – here he observes the conventional reticence of his time in *not* including any account of the seduction; what he does do is to make his heroine's suffering the type of the many. Generally speaking, his commentary is well within character and situation; he rarely makes the personal statement, as in the baptism scene when he says of Tess 'those who knew her' (p. 145). But with Tess's sensitivity and Angel's 'heterodoxy' he is able to make a range of comments within character which may well reflect his own views. There is the celebrated comment on Tess's thoughts and feelings – 'She was expressing in her own native phrases – assisted a little by her Sixth Standard training – feelings which might almost have been called those of the age – the ache of modernism' (p. 180).

Part of Hardy's omniscience is seen in the Biblical and literary analogies which stud the text, often directly relevant as comment on existing situations, sometimes more ornamental or self-indulgent, and reflecting Hardy's particular bias. Saturated in the Bible, Hardy uses Biblical analogy as ironic comment: there are more than a dozen references to Shakespeare's tragedies, a kind of subtext to Tess's; literary references abound, and on one occasion Hardy inverts Browning by having Angel quote, 'with peculiar emendations of his own – "God's *not* in his heaven: all's *wrong* with the world!"' (p. 325)

Arguably this is Angel's consciousness, but we feel the fatalistic authorial tone.

Hardy's own cultural width and his specific interests inform the text. His love of nature is evident throughout, and sometimes this makes for a personal intervention:

She had been told that, rough and brutal as they seemed just then, they were not like this all the year round, but were, in fact, quite civil persons save during certain weeks of autumn and winter, when, like the inhabitants of the Malay Peninsula, they ran amuck, and made it their purpose to destroy life – in this case harmless feathered creatures, brought into being by artificial means solely to gratify these propensities – at once so unmannerly and so unchivalrous towards their weaker fellows in Nature's teeming family. (p. 352)

The analogy is Hardy's, and so is the compassionate tone: if the analogy is outside Tess's range (though this is not certain), the compassion is hers too. But the passage is hardly within her consciousness. Hardy's love of animals is well known (there was a pets' cemetery in the garden of his house) and here, as elsewhere, associations which connect with character or situation in the novel are set up in the reader's mind. The shooting parties are by implication equated with the predatory Alec and the birds with Tess, though their artificial breeding contrasts with her full-blooded nature. I have already mentioned 'the gaunt spectral creatures with tragical eyes' (p. 363) which come to Flintcomb-Ash and there, as here, the individual observation is used to heighten the context.

Most of Hardy's interpolations are brief, and some are inlaid with the kind of reference indicated above. The most celebrated of all begins the final paragraph of the novel. It is worth quoting to underline once more the acuteness of Hardy's revisions. In this instance it marks his determined elevation of Tess's judicial murder to tragic dimensions. It is an irony in itself that the great tragic novelist of the nineteenth century should cite the father of classical tragedy at the conclusion of his narrative. But originally, in the manuscript at the beginning of the last chapter, this omniscient stance is self-conscious: 'The humble delineator of human character and human contingencies, whether his narrative deal with the actual or with the typical only, must primarily and above all things be sincere, however terrible sincerity may be' (*Tess of the d'Urbervilles*, Clarendon Press, 1983, p. 540). This bathos continues for another six lines, but Hardy had sound artistic sense enough to eliminate this. When it came to the final paragraph, however, he used the brief but telling analogy to underline his unequivocal perspective on what his readers had read. The succinctness is masterly, for he goes straight on to the d'Urberville strain, extinct as this pure woman of their line has become extinct: '"Justice" was done, and the President of the Immortals (in Aeschylean phrase) had ended his sport with Tess. And the d'Urberville knights and dames slept on in their tombs unknowing' (p. 489). In the *Graphic* version the bitterness is hidden in a tame phrase after 'Justice was done', 'and Time, the Arch-Satirist, had had his joke out with Tess'. The final version shows Hardy in complete command of commentary: the bitterness is infused with that compassionate irony which embraces the victim of fate. His insistent exposure of man's reduction of woman, or of nature, and of the legal reduction which passes for justice, the rigidity and unfeeling practice of the law, all these reflect a transcendent humanity. I have given a few instances only of his omniscience, aware that his voice is heard throughout the novel; the formal use of that voice, sometimes obtrusive but generally arising out of character and situation, is part of his own deft structure.

6. Themes

There are a number of interrelated themes in *Tess*. 'Phase the Fifth' (see p. 15) is 'The Woman Pays'. There is little doubt that Hardy intends to keep this in the forefront of the reader's mind from the beginning of the novel. We have seen that Tess's short journey through life consists of a series of payments: she pays for her own sense of guilt over the death of Prince, for the loss of innocence and of her child, for the loss of her own peace of mind and social and moral respectability. Throughout her relationship with Angel she pays the price of her secret, and she pays beyond suffering for the revelation of that secret on her wedding night. She pays in toil and tribulation at Flintcomb-Ash, with humility and pride when she visits Angel's parents but fails to see them. She pays by selling herself for her family. She repays, to use a Biblical echo Hardy himself might have employed, when with a vengeance she kills Alec, and then man exacts the ultimate payment, her life. I intend to look at the detail of Tess's payments, but she is not the only woman who pays. Joan Durbeyfield, well versed in the ways of the world, pays for having a shiftless, irresponsible husband and, because he is only a lifeholder, she pays by having to leave her home with her family. She also suffers because of his family pride, through having a large family in economically deprived circumstances; ironic payment is her escape to the alcoholic haze which makes things appear temporarily better than they are.

Throughout the novel the economic dependence of the woman is stressed. By a cunning inversion of his Phase title Hardy makes Joan sell in order to pay. What she sells, not cynically but through preparations on the one hand and discreet silence on the other (though it is hard to think of Joan as either discreet or silent) is her daughter. Here is Tess's departure for Trantridge:

She remained upstairs packing till breakfast-time, and then came down in her ordinary week-day clothes, her Sunday apparel being carefully folded in her box.

Her mother expostulated. 'You will never set out to see your folks without dressing up more the dand than that?'

'But I am going to work!' said Tess.

'Well, yes,' said Mrs Durbeyfield; and in a private tone, 'at first there mid be a little pretence o't ... But I think it will be wiser of 'ee to put your best side outward,' she added.

'Very well; I suppose you know best,' replied Tess with calm abandonment.

And to please her parent the girl put herself quite in Joan's hands, saying serenely – 'Do what you like with me, mother.' (p. 89)

Tess's innocence, her mother's calculation (without fully considering the 'payment' to be exacted from her daughter), Hardy's ease of dialogue here and the use of words like 'abandonment' and 'serenely', all show the ironic emphasis behind the exchange. For Joan, there is the fortune-teller's book and her own romantic temperament to sustain her in hope and support her in adversity. Here the irony of '"Do what you like with me, mother"' is compounded when Sir John is moved to say '"Well, I hope my young friend will like such a comely sample of his own blood. And tell'n, Tess, that being sunk, quite, from our former grandeur, I'll sell him the title – yes, sell it – and at no onreasonable figure"' (p. 91). He has unconsciously forecast her doom.

When Tess returns she is upbraided by her mother for being selfish – even here she has to pay – and Joan tells her, '"I did hope for something to come out o' this! . . . See what he has given us – all, as we thought, because we were his kin. But if he's not, it must have been done because of his love for 'ee. And yet you've not got him to marry!"' (p. 130). The woman who pays daily at the economic level has got her daughter to pay absolutely at the sexual one but, reprimanded by Tess, she becomes more subdued, falling back on '"'Tis nater after all, and what do please God!"' (p. 131). This fatalistic view assumes that the woman pays: Joan's motive for advising her daughter to conceal her past from Angel is clear. But when Angel returns in search of Tess Joan has some inkling of what her daughter has paid. A meddler by nature, she furthers the plot and ensures the final payment.

Marian, Izz and Retty also pay in different kind. So intent is Hardy on demonstrating the subordination of women and their consequent emotional suffering that he has all three milkmaids in love with Angel. Structurally, in a dark parody of this, he also has the Queens of Diamonds and Spades come down in the world at Flintcomb-Ash after their earlier 'phase' of being Alec's mistresses. All payment is relative, but Tess's companions at Talbothays sigh for Angel, kiss his shadow, contrive to be carried by him through the floods and suffer anguish on the day that he is married to Tess. She pays inwardly when she hears how they have reacted: Marian and Retty immediately take to drink, and on his way home a waterman noticed, '"something by the Great Pool; 'twas her bonnet and shawl packed up. In the water he found her. He and another man brought her home, thinking 'a was dead; but she fetched round by degrees"' (p. 289). This is Retty, while Marian is '"found dead drunk by the withy-bed – a girl who hev never been known to touch anything before except shilling ale"' (p. 289). After this she becomes increasingly alcoholic. Izz's payment is the most poignant, and is charged to Angel's impetuosity. He draws from her a confession of love and invites her to accompany him to Brazil. Izz has a searing sense of honesty and pays accordingly. She tells him that nobody could love him as much as Tess does and '"She would have laid down her life for 'ee"' (p. 343). Angel withdraws his offer and passes out of her life: 'she flung herself down on the bank in a fit of racking anguish; and it was with a strained unnatural face that she entered her mother's cottage late that night' (p. 345).

Women pay because they are easily displaced. The field-women at Flintcomb-Ash are employed because they can be paid less than men. Theirs is a life of physical endurance and suffering. Chapter XLIII is testimony to this:

Amid this scene Tess slaved in the morning frosts and the afternoon rains. When it was not swede-grubbing it was swede-trimming, in which process they sliced off the earth and the fibres with a bill-hook before storing the roots for future use. At this occupation they could shelter themselves by a thatched hurdle if it rained; but if it was frosty even their thick leather gloves could not prevent the frozen masses they handled from biting their fingers. (p. 362)

Casual labour means insecurity. On the day of the Durbeyfield 'house-ridding' Marian and Izz move on too, throwing in their lot with a ploughman and his family, for 'It had been a rough life for them at Flintcomb-Ash, and they had come away, almost without notice, leaving Groby to prosecute them if he chose' (p. 445). The narratives of the other women in the novel (Mrs Clare apart) interlock with that of Tess. Hardy's keen sense of the inequality of the sexes, of woman's economic and sexual dependence, is everywhere evident in this, his greatest novel. It would be paradoxical and irrelevant to call him a feminist, and biographers are generally agreed that within his marriages his views could hardly be described as enlightened. But in his fiction his susceptibilities cause him to embrace wider principles and lead here to a positively sympathetic appraisal of the woman's lot. By the time he wrote *Tess* (and we remember the forlorn, forsaken, loyal and deprived Marty South of the previous novel *The Woodlanders*), sympathetic appraisal had taken on the cutting edge of concern. Hardy is not part of a movement; he transcends movements as humanity transcends dogma.

Hardy is of course presenting the double standards of society. The man as sexual sinner goes unpunished by that society, though Alec is killed in terrible retribution by Tess. The statement is clear: man's sexual transgressions are condoned, woman's are condemned. Angel's enlightenment is skin deep, he is incapable of living up to his principles when his wife reveals that she has 'sinned' (she has already forgiven him). This is carefully weighed by Hardy: there is a certain pomposity in Angel's account to Tess of his:

eight-and-forty hours dissipation with a stranger ... 'I would have no more to say to her, and I came home. I have never repeated the offence. But I felt I should like to treat you with perfect frankness and honour, and I could not do so without telling this.' (p. 292)

This precipitates Tess's revelation, her joyful assertion that her offence is 'just the same' (p. 292), a phrase not in the *Graphic*, and Hardy's accompaniment of heavy symbolism prophetic of the dissonance to come. Angel's inadequacy is quite simply the reflection of that wider prejudice and fixed judgement of society. He has confessed, he is clear; she has confessed, she is damned, another person, a deceiver. The irony which informs the double standards is finely focused, for Clare has just helped his bride to that sexual allurement which, society accepted, makes the woman the temptress to whom the man naturally responds:

He suggested to her how to tuck in the upper edge of her bodice, so as to make it roughly approximate to the cut for evening wear; and when she had done this, and the pendant to the necklace hung isolated amid the whiteness of her throat, as it was designed to do, he stepped back to survey her.
'My heavens,' said Clare, 'how beautiful you are!' (p. 287)

And although Angel has moments of compassion after Tess's story, they cannot reconcile him to *his* situation. He feels betrayed, though what happened occurred before he knew Tess: '"You are very good. But it strikes me that there is a want of harmony between your present mood of self-sacrifice and your past mood of self-preservation"' (p. 300).

There is an interesting perspective on social and moral judgement which contrasts with this when Tess returns from Trantridge, is appraised by her friends and then has her baby. She goes to work in the fields, obviously the cynosure of local gossip. She is 'the same, but not the same; at the present stage of her existence living as a stranger and an alien here, though it was no strange land that she was in' (p. 139). The comment is hardly borne out by the little acts of sympathetic acceptance which suggest a community of spirit, a warm concern, from the agricultural workers responding to the fact that one of them has been used and abused. Thus when Tess sits with 'her face turned somewhat away from her companions' a man 'held the cup of ale over the top of the shock for her to drink' (p. 139). This simple gesture is supplemented by the reactions of the men when she begins to feed her baby, those 'who sat nearest considerately turned their faces towards the other end of the field, some of them beginning to smoke; one, with absent-minded fondness, regretfully stroking the jar that would no longer yield a stream' (p. 140). This description is instinct with sympathy and identification, the fondling of the jar having the incipient ambiguity of a reflex loving gesture (as with holding a baby). Perhaps the need for more drink is because of sympathy for Tess. And at this stage rustic commentary takes on a moral, condemnatory, critical and ambivalent view of Tess's case:

'She's fond of that there child, though she mid pretend to hate 'en, and say she wishes the baby and her too were in the churchyard,' observed the woman in the red petticoat.

'She'll soon leave off saying that,' replied the one in buff. 'Lord, 'tis wonderful what a body can get used to o' that sort in time!'

'A little more than persuading had to do wi' the coming o't, I reckon. There were they that heard a sobbing one night last year in The Chase; and it mid ha' gone hard wi' a certain party if folks had come along.'

'Well, a little more or a little less, 'twas a thousand pities that it should have happened to she of all others. But 'tis always the comeliest! The plain ones be as safe as churches . . .' (p. 140)

The combination of forecast (Tess's death-wish is not kept to herself) and the acceptance of suffering, the emphasis that one of their own class is the sufferer, the recognition that the 'comeliest' are likely to be raped, all this exemplifies a broad tolerance and loyalty and freedom from hypocrisy: it contrasts with the double standards of higher society. Tess, whose baby is refused a Christian burial by the vicar, who is later insulted by the man who turns out to be Farmer Groby, whose husband cannot bring himself to stay with her, whose original seducer blackmails her into becoming his mistress, has compensations from her own kind:

Tess's female companions sang songs, and showed themselves very sympathetic and glad at her reappearance out of doors, though they could not refrain from mischievously throwing in a few verses of a ballad about the maid who went to the merry green wood and came back in a changed state. There are counterpoises and compensations in life; and the event which had made of her a social warning had also for the moment made her the most interesting personage in the village to many. Their friendliness won her still further away from herself, their lively spirits were contagious, and she became almost gay. (p. 142)

The use of 'personage' is an ironic register; the ballad and song which are later to be Tess's pathetic connection with the absent Angel are here invoked as humorous and sympathetic rustic comment; best of all, Tess almost, but not quite, laughs at herself. It is one of those rare moments when what she has done is seen from the perspective of self-acceptance rather than blame: generally sorrow is Tess's child in fact and mood.

The reduction of the woman who has sinned by the male who is beyond sin is personified by Farmer Groby, who stands in contradistinction to Dairyman Crick as employer and moral arbiter. The difference is deliberately marked, since Groby is unsympathetic and insulting whereas Crick, ignorant and trusting, is the reverse. Groby's recognition of Tess on Christmas Eve is qualified after Clare strikes him. His explanation is expressive – '"I beg pardon, sir; 'twas a complete mistake. I thought she was another woman, forty miles from here"' (p. 274). In passing we note 'another woman' (how Clare thinks of Tess after her revelation), but the emphasis is on man judging woman for her sin. Groby's own economic subjection of women is degrading by any standards, but there is also Tess's encounter with him (before she knows who he is) on the road to Flintcomb-Ash. He is the 'well-to-do boor' (p. 350) who, having recognized her again, observes '"You ought to beg my pardon for that blow of his, considering"' (p. 350). Caught in the trap of the 'starve-acre' farm and Groby's revenge, Tess learns that although she may not have to fear him sexually, his sadistic streak and social conditioning degrade her: '"Some women are such fools, to take every look as serious earnest. But there's nothing like a winter afield for taking that nonsense out o' young wenches' heads; and you've signed and agreed till Lady-Day. Now, are you going to beg my pardon?"' (p. 367). The repetition of the phrase reflects social divisions and unrelenting moral judgement. Tess has already made a 'mommet' of herself, but the knowledge that she was with Alec d'Urberville and with her 'fancy man', as he feels, ensures his contempt.

The practices of men are accepted and acceptable, given economic power or the spurious status of a Stoke-d'Urberville. The social divisions reflect the moral stances. It is possible to see Cuthbert and Felix Clare as representatives not merely of post-Tractarian Christianity but of mid to late nineteenth-century prejudice. Here is Felix as the brothers see the girls dancing on the green at Marlott: '"Dancing in public with a troop of country hoydens – suppose we should be seen!"' (p. 53). It is the overt respectability which fears contamination, and this is reinforced when, as we have seen, Tess overhears those words to Mercy Chant which show how the brothers view Angel's marriage. He has thrown himself away on a dairymaid and there is little doubt how they, unlike their parents, would view her 'sin'.

Running with smug morality and intolerance is Hardy's antichristian sentiment, which deepens and resonates. There are several crises in which the tone of the author, generally in description, points up the irony of his contemplation. Tess is initially a simple believer (before Angel's rationalism takes hold) who, pursued by her own sin, hastens to obviate that sin by prayer and observance, seen poignantly in the hastily orchestrated baptism of Sorrow. That midnight service sees her, as we have seen, in 'immaculate' prayer and simple ritual emphatic of her purity and sincerity. Hardy observes before this that:

Like all village girls she was well grounded in the Holy Scriptures, and had dutifully studied the histories of Aholah and Aholibah, and knew the inferences to be drawn therefrom. But when the same question arose with regard to the baby, it had a very different colour. Her darling was about to die, and no salvation. (p. 143)

The reference to Ezekiel and the punishment of two whores by God is ironic in view of Tess's feverish anxiety. The reference has a fire and brimstone fearfulness which takes no account of humility, repentance, forgiveness. Tess's imagination sees her child as

consigned to the nethermost corner of hell, as its double doom for lack of baptism and lack of legitimacy; saw the arch-fiend tossing it with his three-pronged fork, like the one they used for heating the oven on baking days; to which picture she added many other quaint and curious details of torment sometimes taught the young in this Christian country. (p. 143)

It is in this anguish that Tess baptizes Sorrow, and Hardy, as if unable to let go of Christianity's limitations, has Tess ask the parson if her service will be '"just the same for him as if you had baptized him"' (p. 146). Hardy's immediate analogy indicates his own condescension towards the practices of the Church and the acceptance of them by those who conform. I repeat the quotation here because of its force and effect:

Having the natural feelings of a tradesman at finding that a job he should have been called in for had been unskilfully botched by his customers among themselves, he was disposed to say no. Yet the dignity of the girl, the strange tenderness in her voice, combined to affect his nobler impulses – or rather those that he had left in him after ten years of endeavour to graft technical belief on actual scepticism. The man and the ecclesiastic fought within him, and the victory fell to the man.

'My dear girl,' he said, 'it will be just the same.' (p. 147)

But this humane reflex is tested even further when Tess presses him to give the baby a Christian burial. His reply of '"I must not – for certain reasons"' provokes Tess's impulsive '"and I'll never come to your church no more"' (p. 147). Again the parson compromises his faith in the interests of his humanity, assuring Tess that it will be just the same as far as the baby is concerned as if he had done it.

Hardy's expressive anti-dogmatic sentiments do not undermine his heroine's beliefs, and after her long 'reconstructive' period Tess, when she enters the Vale of Blackmoor, chants the psalter instead of 'several ballads', though she pauses after the praise of God to say, '"But perhaps I don't quite know the Lord as yet"' (p. 158). This follows Hardy's 'The Froom waters were clear as the pure River of Life shown to the Evangelist' (p. 157) in Revelation.

I have said that Hardy's irony lies in the fact that his concern with religious practice is constantly underpinned by wide-ranging Biblical reference throughout the text. It would be true to say that there are pivotal moments in the plot in which Hardy's own tolerance redresses the balance of his bias. Angel Clare rejects ordination, but his pompous self-justification does not endear him to the reader, although his idea that his education should be used '"for the honour and glory of man"' (p. 171) is a noble one. Hardy's account of Mr Clare carries a degree of warmth as well as an unvoiced criticism of those churchmen who lack his faith: 'He was a man not merely religious, but devout; a firm believer – not as the phrase is now exclusively construed by theological thimble-riggers in the Church and out of it, but in the old and ardent sense of the Evangelical school ...' (pp. 170–71). Mr Clare endures insults from Alec (and others) and, though severe, is sincere, practical, fearless. There is no condescension in Hardy's presentation, merely recognition of what is essentially good even if somewhat blinkered.

Other religious references involve the sign-painter, who has already been considered in relation to Tess. His warnings echo the baptism scene, and the same hell-fire associations are present in the old woman's account of Alec's preaching. Tess's view of the convert and the extreme nature of the ranting is seen in the presence of 'the man whom she had seen carrying the red paint-pot on a former memorable occasion' (p. 380). He is not in the audience in the *Graphic* version. Once again

Hardy's telling insertion marks his emphasis in moral stance and literary structure.

Tess's reaction to Alec's preaching is inward but cynically expressive, one feels, of Hardy's views – 'The greater the sinner the greater the saint; it was not necessary to dive far into Christian history to discover that' (p. 384). But Tess's acceptance of Clare's views, which supplanted her simple beliefs, is also subjected to ironic appraisal which is scarcely less direct than that which comments on the limitations of the Church and Christianity. Alec tells Tess, not without some truth, '"A pretty fellow he must be to teach you such scepticism!"' (p. 400). In the *Graphic* the last word was 'subjection', an interesting variant on Tess's subordination to Angel. But when Tess says, '"He said at another time something like this"; and she gave another, which might possibly have been paralleled in many a work of the pedigree ranging from the *Dictionnaire Philosophique* to Huxley's *Essays*' (pp. 400–401), we feel the pathos rather than the substance of what Tess is saying. We feel too Hardy's irony, that the views of the egoist and the sceptic are not necessarily an improvement on, say, the views (and practices) of Mr Clare. Angel is not an improvement on his father. He is arguably a lesser man, less tolerant, less charitable, less forgiving. Hardy's concern is to expose and diminish dogma which lacks human flexibility. Blind adherence to dogma, Christian or otherwise, like blind acceptance of the machinery of tne law, attracts his criticism. Tess, overvaluing Angel's views as she does, obviously expresses views with which Hardy is in full agreement. She says, '"I believe in the *spirit* of the Sermon on the Mount, and so did my dear husband . . . But I don't believe –"' Here she gave her negations' (p. 400). Almost inevitably, I suppose, from 'But' onwards was not in the *Graphic*, though even with 'negations' it seems that Tess is being reticent. He may also have seen of course that for Tess to reject everything specifically that she had hitherto accepted would be a diminishing, a reduction to unthinking nullity. Once more the reply from the convert has some truth in it, despite Hardy's care: '"whatever your dear husband believed you accept, and whatever he rejected you reject, without the least inquiry on your own part. That's just like you women. Your mind is enslaved to his"' (p. 400). At one time in his young manhood Hardy considered entering the Church. *Tess* is saturated with religious reference and innuendo, and it is the saturation of the one-time student and sympathizer. But life has taken Hardy beyond God and back to man or, more accurately, to woman. He sees, with the clear-sightedness which comes from experience and self-evaluation, that rejection and denial do not answer without humanity, tolerance and understanding. Though *Tess* confronts its own time, its concerns are with intolerance, rigidity that passes for morality and dogmatic observances that pass for religion. And no theories can replace humanity, for humanity comes from the kind of life experiences that cause the 'large-minded stranger' to tell Clare in Brazil that 'What Tess had been was of no importance beside what she would be' (p. 422).

J. R. Ebbatson* has correctly (as it seems to me) observed of Tess that 'the articulation of the nature theme in the novel stands creatively poised between images of romantic pastoral and scientific battleground'. And he adds that 'The protagonists ... are unwilling agents of evolutionary change.' Hardy's irony embraces the pastoral settings – the obviously contrasting ones of Talbothays and Flintcomb-Ash, for example – but each is inlaid with the Darwinian struggle, the law of survival and sexual selection. The romantic idyll is undermined by outsiders like Alec and Angel, both of whom reduce nature (Tess) just as the machine traps and kills animals. The influence of Darwinian thought is apparent in the novel and in Hardy's deliberate patterning of the pastoral and the rational, the factual and the romantic.

Of the many ironies that run through *Tess*, one of the most interesting is that of deception and its corollary of self-deception. Much of its dramatic intensity is seen in Tess's unintentional and then vacillating deception of Angel about her past. It is seen in Angel's self-deception, his belief in his own moral enlightenment, which proves to be based on the shifting sands of his own self-pride. It is seen in Alec's deception of Tess, which ironically begins with his being a Stoke-d'Urberville and not the descendant of the authentic dynasty. Tess's father is the debased and self-deceiving representative of that, while his wife is reprimanded by Tess for failing to tell her – for deceiving her – about what men are like: '"Why didn't you warn me! Ladies know what to fend hands against, because they read novels that tell them of these tricks; but I never had the chance o' learning in that way, and you did not help me!"' (p. 131). The irony of contrasting raw life with behaviour in society novels will not be lost on the reader of *Tess*, which links structurally the many strands of human deception. They are apparent, I suggest, early in the novel, where Parson Tringham unwittingly deceives Durbeyfield by telling him of his forebears, by calling him 'Sir John', and by inadvertently raising false expectations in this already weak and

*'A Darwinian Version of Pastoral – Hardy's *Tess*', in Bryan Loughrey, ed., *Pastoral Mode*, Macmillan, 1984 (Macmillan Casebook). Adapted from Chapter 4 of Roger Ebbatson's *Lawrence and the Nature Tradition*, Harvester Press, 1983.

vacillating man, for whom self-deception now becomes obsessive. Tringham knows, or fears, what he has done, and Durbeyfield's response is immediately to give himself airs – '"And when you've done that go on to my house with the basket, and tell my wife to put away that washing, because she needn't finish it, and wait till I come home, as I've news to tell her"' (p. 47). A knighthood, however spurious, lifts one above mundane things. In 'Sir John's' case it lifts him into Rolliver's and renders him unfit to take the hives. Rolliver's itself is a low-key echo of the major deceptions: the landlady is self-rehearsed in the phrase she needs to prove her innocence should '"any member of the Gover'ment"' be passing, '"Being a few private friends I've asked in to keep up club-walking at my own expense"' (p. 64). It is here that the deception of Tess begins, with Joan announcing her 'projick' to send Tess to her relations at Trantridge. Hardy investigates the Stoke-d'Urbervilles, tracing the line whose name is calculated to deceive the simple and opportunistic Joan. On arrival and seeing the place, Tess in her 'artlessness' unconsciously identifies the deception – '"I thought we were an old family; but this is all new!"' (p. 77). Hardy's own definition derives from the forgery of Mr Simon Stoke: he fancied the name of d'Urberville which 'was annexed to his own name for himself and his heirs eternally. Yet he was not an extravagant-minded man in this, and in constructing his family tree on the new basis was duly reasonable in framing his intermarriages and aristocratic links, never inserting a single title above a rank of strict moderation' (p. 78). The last sentence, with its unequivocal moral emphasis and its acute sense of the meretricious nature of class distinction, was not in the *Graphic*.

Tess, with her capacity for dreaming, is a self-deceiver too, and when she first sees Alec the difference between his reality and her conception is marked – 'She had dreamed of an aged and dignified face, the sublimation of all the d'Urberville lineaments, furrowed with incarnate memories representing in hieroglyphic the centuries of her family's and England's history' (p. 79). Hardy's emphases early on foreshadow the clear track of plot and situation – life is the arch-deceiver, our expectations are themselves a deception, and that experience is reality *and* deception at one and the same time. The full expression of deception is manifest, particularly when we consider Hardy's explanatory note to the first edition where he speaks of being able to 'piece the trunk and limbs of the novel together'. First of all Tess deceives Alec about the baby. It is an early sign of that intense pride which drives her in upon herself, and is seen in the periodic recurrence to the death-wish. After the long period of recovery, she decides to become a milkmaid at a distance, and to conceal her past and her ancestry. When Crick refers to the '"family of some such name as yours"' (pp. 161–2) and their ancient lineage, Tess keeps quiet. As she draws closer to Angel, Hardy stresses the risk she is taking when he says, 'Tess was trying to lead a repressed life, but she little divined the strength of her own vitality' (p. 181). Everything at Talbothays conspires to make her keep up the deception and although she determines to tell Angel about her past she can't. She is fearful even of a public denunciation 'on the grounds of her history' (p. 271). Yet when we consider the fate of the letter she sends Angel we know that her deception is inadvertent when she gets closer to marriage. And when she hears Angel's confession she deceives herself– but how rightly! – that what she has done is just the same. In essence it is, but she deceives herself in thinking that Angel will see it that way.

Her own capacity for self-deception continues. She idealizes and idolizes Angel throughout the first period of his absence. She deceives herself, at least in part, about her ability to withstand the determined persuasions of Alec. Clare, as we have seen, is self-deceived in his relations with Tess. He is deceived in seeing what he wants to see in her rather than what she is, deceiving himself by thinking of the image and not searching the reality. In a sense, the most terrible moment in his deception is his invitation to Izz: his retraction shows how cruel the deception has been. But the overall deception in *Tess* is shown in Hardy's presentation of his society. The Church and the law, for example, are deceptive, deceiving and flawed. The emphasis is microcosmic; the deceptions and self-deceptions of individuals are mirrored in a world which deceives.

Fate and coincidence, linked to the superstitions and traditions which influence character, are of primary importance in any Hardy novel. In *Tess* they predominate, from the broad conception down to the smallest details. Coincidence or determinism, with an overview that predetermines (or seems to), omniscient (from Hardy) and omniscient (from the 'President of the Immortals'), all cohere to make *Tess* a profoundly disturbing novel. This is not just because of Hardy's views but more because we recognize in the fictional pattern he presents an equivalence in our own lives. The pattern from Tringham's revelation, through Tess wistfully gazing at the unknown Angel Clare, through her self-accusation over the dead Prince, her staying at Trantridge, the fateful (my word) night when she is 'rescued' by Alec from his cast-off mistresses, all this is bald plot statement. Narrative art imposes on this the similitude of life, records the chance situations which life records too. Life, like a novel, is a plot: caught up in it, we see it as evolving from situation to situation, sometimes easily predictable, sometimes not. In the novel it is true to say that Tess sees herself as fated from the death of Prince onwards. Hardy operates successfully between a naturalistic conception of an evolving destiny, made by chance, location, coincidence, for example, and an unseen destiny which seems to oversee and orchestrate everything that happens. The two are not incompatible: in fact they are so integrated as to be inseparable at times in the narrative.

The first involves the exercise of volition in life or in the fiction which represents life. The second is a belief in or an acceptance of fate which exists above and beyond individuals in fiction or in life. Almost from the first, Tess seems fated in everything she does. Let us take briefly the incidents mentioned above. Tringham's meeting with her father sets off Joan's opportunism; the coincidence of meeting Angel some years later is enhanced by her *not* being the one he notices here, whereas at Talbothays he notices her particularly. The spiking of Prince (remember that Tess had dozed off, though her morbid fear of fate had been shown in her conversation with Abraham) leads her to consider herself a murderess. She is 'fated' to become one. Her visit to Trantridge ensures her fate.

So far, apart from Tess's inward apprehensions, the outward events are seen as potent indicators of malign fate – the mail-cart, for example, and Alec's opportunism, his being in the right place at the right time. If we go on, we find the inexorable nature of fate (or Hardy's plotting) continues her reduction. There is her love–hate for the baby, the death of Sorrow, the time for recovery. The signs are auspicious. The Phase title is 'The Rally', Talbothays is outwardly fair and companionable, but soon the fateful pressures begin to accumulate within. The meeting with Angel means the tighter inward hugging of her secret, the Jack Dollop stories reflect her fears, the developing love for Angel, and a host of incidents attendant upon that which we have already considered, all combine to inflict Tess's fate upon her. The d'Urberville portraits and the legend of the coach, the afternoon crow and the behaviour of the other girls on the wedding day, all these show Hardy presenting fate as an accumulation of circumstances. Arising naturally, their overall effect is that of a malign Fate stalking its victim, and the theme of a victim – supplemented by a commentary on social morality – is also central in *Tess*. We are aware of an inexorable pressure from which there is no escape. Although 'Too Late Beloved' would have been an inadequate and tasteless title (though having perhaps a romantic irony) it does in fact emphasize an important part of the plot which derives from fate. Thus Angel's realization of how he has treated Tess comes too late, to take an obvious example. In fact everything comes too late, like Tess's retreat from Trantridge, Joan's failure (deliberate) to warn her daughter about men, her second meeting with Alec (too late to counteract the consequences of the first) and, above all, her confession to Angel. Hardy is not merely recording the mechanism of coincidence, but also showing the human temptations and errors which make us victims. And this is where, in this novel particularly, the outward and the inward cohere. The might-have-been element which is present in the projected title impregnates *Tess*.

The Flintcomb-Ash sequence leads to a number of fateful experiences. Take, for instance, the arrival of Izz (how ironic to want to live the happy old times together!), her revelations to Marian and Marian's telling Tess of Angel's invitation to Izz. It provokes Tess to visit Emminster: Hardy's notation here stresses the accident of chronology – 'It was a year ago, all but a day, that Clare had married Tess, and only a few days less than a year that he had been absent from her' (p. 373). We have already noted the Cross-in-Hand sequence, and Hardy loads Tess's journey with an oppression of fateful incident – the changing of the boots for the 'pretty thin ones of patent leather', Tess's feelings, the ringing of the doorbell without response, the whipping up of the ivy-leaves, and 'the piece of blood-stained paper' (p. 374), the movement away from the house and the emotional index which charts her fears – 'A feeling haunted her that she might have been recognized (though how she could not tell), and orders been given not to admit her' (p. 375). All this maintains the temperature of narrative which suggests the fated victim. And the might-have-been fate is present too, not just in commentary but in the implicit recognition that Tess is an enemy to herself because of her susceptibility. When she overhears Angel's brothers discussing her and Angel she is so grief-stricken and bitter that she sets off for Flintcomb-Ash without trying to see Mr and Mrs Clare. Hardy's suggestion is that they would have welcomed her and comforted her *because* she was a sinner. There is too an unvoiced but fatal emphasis between the lines: she would not then have met Alec again. The course of her history might have taken a different direction. As it is, the combination of incidents precipitates her tragedy. Her life is of course predetermined by her creator, but Hardy manages to inject into the narrative the idea that what she does not do influences her fate as much as what she does do. She says of her own looks '"It is nothing – it is nothing . . . Nobody loves it; nobody sees it. Who cares about the looks of a castaway like me!"' (p. 378). It is bitterly said, but some hours later – as fate decrees – she is face to face with someone who does care, not the beloved conventional man but the agent of her double destruction – her fate – the 'converted' Alec d'Urberville.

Fate now becomes subsumed in blackmail, with Angel's silence and the family crisis an emotional coercion. On the last night in the house where she and the children were born Tess comforts her brothers and sisters. They sing words they have learned at Sunday school: these words subserve the fate/victim theme:

> Here we suffer grief and pain,
> Here we meet to part again;
>   In Heaven we part no more. (p. 441)

The irony informs this as it informs the whole conception of *Tess*. It seems confirmation to Tess of her own role as victim, and she has just impulsively written to Angel '"You are cruel, cruel indeed! I will try to forget you. It is all injustice I have received at your hands! T."' (p. 440). Tess has her own crisis of faith exacerbated by the children's words. She puts it in this way to herself and in doing so points herself in the direction of Alec:

If she could only believe what the children were singing; if she were only sure, how different all would now be; how confidently she would leave them to Providence . . . (p. 441)

But she is fated 'to be their Providence' (p. 441). And at this stage, as we have seen, she recurs to her earlier fate, convincing herself that 'this man alone was her husband' (p. 442). She is willing her own future fate because of her husband's silence, her family's deprivation and her own capacity for self-blame, coming to feel she deserves the punishment she gets.

Minor fateful occurrences qualify the departure and the arrival. There is the meeting with Marian and Izz (they write to Angel), there is her mother's booking of the rooms (too late) at Kingsbere, the arrival at the family vault, the manifestation of Alec. Though Tess here wishes for death she is destined to live through the worst that fate can offer. Angel wills himself to return, but his own obstinacy and illness retard his return until too late. The final comment in the novel, and indeed the whole of the last chapter, underlines Hardy's conception that we are all victims of fate, that we are predestined to particular roles in life; sometimes we may have the will to effect change, but we don't – or can't. The conversation between Tess and Abraham (pp. 69–70) has been given much attention in this context, and it still repays a close look. Tess is tired and a little irritable, and Abraham is pestering her, a miniature of the type of pestering she is to endure over the d'Urbervilles, to which Abraham has already drawn her attention earlier in the conversation. The reference to the apples and her father's tipsiness is part of her mood, made worse by Abraham's remark about her marrying a gentleman. The accident comes about as a result of her dreaming. The implication is perhaps that fate takes us unaware, but it is also surely that had Tess been awake the accident would not have happened and her course in life would have been different. The might-have-been stress is therefore a major factor in the omnipresence of fate near the beginning of the novel. Tess's withdrawal, understandable in view of her exhaustion, leads to the fateful consequences, both here and later. After she has contemplated Prince and condemned herself for dancing the previous day and regarded herself as a murderess, Abraham acts as chorus on her inner state – ' " " 'Tis because we are on a blighted star, and not a sound one, isn't it, Tess?" ' (p. 72). But we must weigh Tess's overreaction in the balance of fate. Because of her sensitivity she is always inviting self-injury. On one occasion she expresses regret to Angel that he did not stay and love her when she was sixteen – before fate intervened, is her silent thought. Angel reassures her and adds:

'But you must not be so bitter in your regret – why should you be?'

With the woman's instinct to hide she diverged hastily –

'I should have had four years more of your heart than I can ever have now. Then I should not have wasted my time as I have done – I should have had so much longer happiness!'

It was no mature woman with a long dark vista of intrigue behind her who was tormented thus; but a girl of simple life, not yet one-and-twenty, who had been caught during her days of immaturity like a bird in a springe. To calm herself the more completely she rose from her little stool and left the room, overturning the stool with her skirts as she went. (p. 261)

This combination of dialogue and commentary reveals and exposes Tess as victim of fate. In looking so often to the past she unbalances herself in the present. She is fearful of speaking out and perhaps bringing a worse fate upon herself. She is, so to speak, her own fate. She courts it again by writing to her mother, knowing only too well that she will be told to go on keeping her secret. In a burst of courage she confronts her fate directly. Her letter to Angel is her confession; fate, in the shape of the carpet, intervenes. She is doomed from within and without: 'With a feeling of faintness she withdrew the letter. There it was – sealed up, just as it had left her hands. The mountain had not yet been removed' (p. 277). She tries to climb it before they are married, fails and leaves it too late. Again the might-have-been which is part of Tess's fate is present. She withdraws into dream or reverie, perhaps a deliberate retreat from fate, understandable but culpable. Hardy puts it in convoluted prose which neatly reflects the confused and apprehensive nature of Tess's thoughts and feelings: 'In dressing she moved about in a mental cloud of many-coloured idealities, which eclipsed all sinister contingencies by its brightness' (p. 278).

7. The Past and the Present

Although the chronology of *Tess* is straightforward, the influence of the past on the present in personal and social ways is of great importance. Hardy establishes a continuity of tradition as well as a notation of change, the movement down of old families and the movement up of new. Tess is not the only character whose inheritance has changed. The history of Retty Priddle and the corruption of her name is similar to that of the d'Urbervilles. Dairyman Crick, who presumably is *not* descended from an ancient family, is a character who links past and present with his tales and a width of local reference. Present gossip supplements past tradition in his unreflecting fluency. He draws Tess's attention to Angel's dislike of old families – '"He says that ... old families ... can't have anything left in them now"' (p. 183) – and draws the parallel with Retty unconsciously: '"Why, our little Retty Priddle here, you know, is one of the Paridelles – the old family that used to own lots o' lands out by King's-Hintock now owned by the Earl o' Wessex, afore even he or his was heard of"' (pp. 183–4). The caricature of what Angel thinks is so close to Tess's own family state that it further undermines her.

Hardy's simple formula is to refer quite often to the d'Urberville past and compare it with the degraded d'Urberville present. This he does at crisis points in the narrative, from the first meeting with Parson Tringham right through to the expressive irony of the last paragraph, 'And the d'Urberville knights and dames slept on in their tombs unknowing' (p. 489). I say irony because the past is never buried, particularly in the case of Tess: it is only sublimated, and then not very successfully. The influence of her past 'family', its fall, correlates with her own past, her fall. Everything happens between the 'how are the mighty fallen' (quoted by Tringham) at the beginning to the mighty fallen (in their tombs) and the humble fallen (Sir John and Tess) at the end. Obviously the stress mark of fate, as we have said, is seen in the past and the present. Situations which are comparable occur in each, and we have noted that the forcing of Tess provokes Hardy to comment on the fact that her ancestors doubtless 'dealt the same measure even more ruthlessly towards the peasant girls of their time' (p. 119).

The interlocking of past and present is, as I have said, treated

102

ironically by Hardy, perhaps nowhere more so than in the false pride of John Durbeyfield over the burial of Prince, when he refers to the 'chargers' kept by his ancestors. In the present he has done little to support his family, and the irony notes the economic suffering of the family, which might have suffered less if he had been ignorant of the past.

The d'Urberville presence is a potent force in Tess's present, witness the story of the d'Urberville coach and the encroaching influence of the family portraits in the farmhouse-mansion. The fall from mansion to farmhouse parallels the fall of the family: and since it is the scene of Tess's confession, its influence on Clare is understandable. He breaks out in condemnation of old families in almost the way reported by Crick earlier:

'Decrepit families imply decrepit wills, decrepit conduct. Heaven, why did you give me a handle for despising you more by informing me of your descent! Here was I thinking you a new-sprung child of nature; there were you, the belated seedling of an effete aristocracy!' (p. 302)

Clare is perhaps surprisingly fluent for an overwrought man, but by his standards fate – and the past – has played him a cruel trick. Her past efforts to tell him of her past, plus her own determination at one stage to shut out that past – have now brought them to an intolerable present. We remember in the light of this the earlier irony:

'I – I am not a Durbeyfield, but a d'Urberville – a descendant of the same family as those that owned the old house we passed. And – we are all gone to nothing!'

'A d'Urberville! – Indeed! And is that all the trouble, dear Tess?'

'Yes,' she answered faintly.

'Well – why should I love you less after knowing this?'

'I was told by the dairyman that you hated old families' . . .

She had not told. At the last moment her courage had failed her, she feared his blame for not telling him sooner . . . (pp. 252–3)

The personal past and the inherited past are here brought into inter-action.

The influence of the past on the present is seen in Alec d'Urberville. Tess, we remember, did not tell him when she left Trantridge that she was going to have a baby. He re-enters Tess's life when, in a curiously ironic way, Tess is able to make some reparation to her family for having failed them (as she believes) in the past. Hardy, as I have said, puts Alec in a number of physical stances in relation to Tess, the meeting at the vault with its death suggestions (reminiscences too of herself, Angel and the stone coffin) being particularly effective. Tess sees a recumbent figure. In the dusk she had not noticed it before, and would hardly have noticed it now but for an odd fancy that the effigy moved. As soon as she drew close to it she discovered all in a moment that the figure was a living person. (p. 449)

We remember that Angel's placing of Tess in the coffin was, in crudely symbolic terms, an anticipation of her placing herself on the sacrificial stone at Stonehenge. Here the force of the revelation that the living person is Alec is not merely to fix the death associations with Tess. It is surely to emphasize that Alec 'living' – a modern d'Urberville more potent than her ancestors – ensures that her past will live on too. Having failed her family in the past she is now exposed to the extremity of blackmail in their and her deteriorating present. It would be wrong to deny that we feel the contrivance of the situation, the irrevocable and fatalistic power: but it is a masterstroke of structure at the same time. In expressing Tess's fate, Hardy here brings together the historical past and the personal past, the decay of d'Urbervilles to Durbeyfields, or the worse decadence of buying your past through a name and stamping it on the present as a seal. Throughout this treatment of the past in the present Hardy emphasizes that Tess is not decadent: it is simply that present events are too much for her, and that she cannot integrate her past into them *in her own mind*.

8. Backgrounds and Movements

Hardy's Wessex is rightly celebrated for its important functions in his novels, and I do not intend here to consider identifications or tracings or basic map work. Backgrounds in Hardy are strictly foregrounds of tradition, convention, superstition, gossip, everything which makes the ethos authentic against the natural verisimilitude. The agricultural workers, both male and female, are presented as relying on what they can get from seasonal work. The women in particular are seen as migratory. Pleasure is occasionally unconfined as compensation, as the Chaseborough sequence implies – Hardy's description is graphic, conveying the frenzy of workpeople released from drudgery:

The movements grew more passionate: the fiddlers behind the luminous pillar of cloud now and then varied the air by playing on the wrong side of the bridge or with the back of the bow. But it did not matter; the panting shapes spun onwards. (p. 108)

The sequence is punctuated by dancing, drinking, arguments, falling over and as we see from Tess's experience shortly afterwards, the threat of violence.

The work experience of the women at Flintcomb-Ash is stultifying, monotonous; take the piece-work in Groby's barn:

Putting on their gloves all set to work in a row in front of the press, an erection formed of two posts connected by a cross-beam, under which the sheaves to be drawn from were laid ears outward, the beam being pegged down by pins in the uprights and lowered as the sheaves diminished. (p. 366)

The *Graphic* version included more technical detail obviously cut here in the interests of narrative tension, since the two 'Amazonian sisters' from Chaseborough are present and we wonder if they will eventually recognize Tess. Again Hardy's social concerns are evident in his brief account of them:

They did all kinds of men's work by preference, including well-sinking, hedging, ditching, and excavating, without any sense of fatigue. Noted reed-drawers were they too, and looked round upon the other three with some superciliousness. (p. 366)

105

These are heavy tasks, but even heavier is the burden which falls upon Tess, allegedly selected by Groby for her strength and quickness in feeding the machine:

The hum of the thresher, which prevented speech, increased to a raving whenever the supply of corn fell short of the regular quantity. As Tess and the man who fed could never turn their heads she did not know that just before the dinner-hour a person had come silently into the field by the gate . . . (pp. 406–7)

Apart from the symbolic (and physical) trapping of Tess between the two, the work represents the power and demands of the machine, the increasing mechanization indicating the movement away from tradition. The background may be permanent, but lives are changed. Here the machine dominates the day, its 'inexorable wheels' going non-stop apart from breaks and, as I have suggested earlier, it is the symbolic accompaniment of fate.

But whether the scene is the lush pasture of Talbothays or the ice-bound bleakness of Flintcomb-Ash, the cheap labour of women and the particular tasks for men remain despite the machines. The rural way of the world goes on, and the class divisions of the world into which Tess was born are integral to its ethos. The class background of Tringham, the Clares and the parson at Marlott is that of the superior group which works with its head (particularly in matters of faith) and not with its hands for sustenance. These class divisions are part of Hardy's moral commentary, and it is interesting that there is a deliberate contrast between Clare and d'Urberville as 'new' men, though different in moral texture. In her relationship with each of them Tess is displaced from her class. She is not one of the 'troop of country hoydens' referred to by Felix with passing condescension, but she cannot enter the lower professional class despite her achievements in school and her potential. There is the suggestion that she would be more than a farmer's wife under the stimulus of Angel's tutelage. Hardy's ironic appraisal of Angel and Alec shows his awareness of class movements. Alec has taken the d'Urberville name and the class assumptions that go with it: he is a throwback to them therefore in an ironic sense. Clare, the agnostic, represents a new generation, moving from the professional class into the farming, commercial class, from the spiritual to the practical. Yet he too reverts to the old standards in his relations with Tess, even to the appreciation of her ancestry. Interestingly, Alec is indolent (apart from his ephemeral conversion) while we feel that Angel's idea of farming is largely in the head. Hardy's appraisal of class divisions is seen directly in Angel's words to the suffering Tess:

'For your own sake I rejoice in your descent. Society is hopelessly snobbish, and this fact of your extraction may make an appreciable difference to its acceptance of you as my wife, after I have made you the well-read woman I mean to make you. My mother too, poor soul, will think so much better of you on account of it. Tess, you must spell your name correctly – d'Urberville – from this very day.' (pp. 253–4)

This tells us much of Clare but even more of society. The farmer taking as his wife someone who can help to run things from practical knowledge is here subsumed by his inherited class prejudices and conditioning. His condescension and family awareness show how completely trapped he is. Angel is much more conventional and of his time than he knows. Hardy is showing that real, positive movement is limited. Tess's mother recognizes this, knowing that her daughter's best chance of acceptance into a different class is to remain silent. Appearance is so much more important than reality.

Throughout this study I have emphasized Hardy's sense of structure at all levels of the narrative, through character, image, symbol, the incidence of fate and the past and the present, for example. Parallel and contrast are of the essence, and this is seen in the presentation of background and its interaction with character, as I indicated at the beginning of this section. Marlott and Trantridge–Chaseborough provide early contrasts in the novel, with Tess trapped economically in the first, sexually in the second, then returning to the first to have her child before reconstructing her life and going to Talbothays (though there is a period near Port Bredy). When she goes to Talbothays she negotiates the Vale of Blackmoor after descending 'the Egdon slopes lower and lower towards the dairy of her pilgrimage' (p. 158). I have said earlier that the word 'pilgrimage' gives Tess's journeys a spiritual and moral weighting, and this is true in terms of atmosphere and mood in her movement to Talbothays. Simply, nature is lush and various, there is hope and companionship, the 'Rally' is characterized by love and Tess's fullness of nature despite the inhibitions of the past. There is a very strong identification with nature, seen in the description of the cows, full, imaginative, loving, lingering:

while the sun, lowering itself behind this patient row, threw their shadows accurately inwards upon the wall . . . Those of them that were spotted with white reflected the sunshine in dazzling brilliancy, and the polished brass knobs on their horns glittered with something of military display. Their large-veined udders hung ponderous as sandbags, the teats sticking out like the legs of a gypsy's crock; and as each animal lingered for her turn to arrive the milk oozed forth and fell in drops to the ground. (p. 160)

The metaphorical lushness matches that of the place and the beasts. Hardy seems – like Tess – to be motivated into a higher style which has its equivalence in season and location. And added to this is Hardy's consummate particularity; at Talbothays the expanse of exterior – freedom – is balanced by the sympathetic examination of interior – domestic life, love, emotion. Angel is described as having a strong dislike of town life and a feeling for the countryside, hence his occupational choice. As student rather than just workman he is given

an immense attic which ran the whole length of the dairy-house. It could only be reached by a ladder from the cheese-loft, and had been closed up for a long time till he arrived and selected it as his retreat. Here Clare had plenty of space, and could often be heard by the dairy-folk pacing up and down when the household had gone to rest. (p. 172)

This particularity or exactitude is part of Hardy's practical awareness translated into literary expression. The word 'retreat' picks up 'pilgrimage' in a way, though we note that soon Clare's restlessness and harp-strumming give way to an enjoyment of the working company in the 'general dining-kitchen' (p. 173). In general terms the sympathetic backgrounds of exterior and interior are responsible for bringing Angel and Tess together. The interior at times is almost erotically claustrophobic. The mornings, cool, with even a fire in the breakfast-room, are wonderfully evoked in terms of the close companionship and response. Outside, the companionship of the cows and *their* responses and preferences are given a considered weight, not so much sentimentalized as real in the ambience of developing experience, a bovine yielding as tremulous as the human one. The atmosphere is generative, but Hardy goes beyond sympathy to mutability. The following passage, often quoted, is the symbolic connective with man and woman – here *the* man and *the* woman – and nature. It is more evidence of Hardy's structural deliberateness:

The season developed and matured. Another year's instalment of flowers, leaves, nightingales, thrushes, finches, and such ephemeral creatures, took up their positions where only a year ago others had stood in their place when these were nothing more than germs and inorganic particles. Rays from the sunrise drew forth the buds and stretched them into long stalks, lifted up sap in noiseless streams, opened petals, and sucked out scents in invisible jets and breathings. (p. 185)

David Skilton points out that this cyclical process fascinated Hardy, the first part here being virtually transcribed into his poem 'Proud

Songsters', which was published in 1928. I feel that the precise focus here connects directly with Tess, Angel, the nature of life and love, with certain words evocatively stretched to suggest associations in the wider text of the novel. For example, 'instalment' seems oddly poised here, until we remember that it means 'payment' as well as 'part', thus sounding a theme. The emphasis on the 'ephemeral creatures' looks across at Tess and her short existence, and is in any case a reminder that she is often compared to creatures. Nature is as vulnerable as she is. There is too a certain erotic element in the description typical of Hardy's symbolic use of background. Sexuality permeates the Talbothays experience, Tess coming naturally into greater fullness of nature and Angel responding (at times) to her proximity. Hardy indicates Tess's warmth of response directly, and links her at once with nature:

Tess had never in her recent life been so happy as she was now, possibly never would be so happy again. She was, for one thing, physically and mentally suited among these new surroundings. The sapling which had rooted down to a poisonous stratum on the spot of its sowing had been transplanted to a deeper soil. (p. 185)

The analogy of Tess's nature with Nature underlines her transformation after the Trantridge seduction and the Marlott misery, those backgrounds inhibiting or injuring natural growth. Here at Talbothays Tess grows – she expands into physical, mental, emotional fullness, which is only threatened by her past, her incipient sense of guilt. And the foreground, the interior, is conducive to the development of love, of greater fulfilment, this last word chosen despite Hardy's ironic use of it as the final phase title: 'No sooner had the hour of three struck and whizzed, than she left the room and ran to the dairyman's door; then up the ladder to Angel's, calling him in a loud whisper; then woke her fellow-milkmaids' (p. 186).

The interior is shared in such a way as to promote intimacy:

Being so often – possibly not always by chance – the first two persons to get up at the dairy-house they seemed to themselves the first persons up of all the world. In these early days of her residence here Tess did not skim, but went out of doors at once after rising, where he was generally awaiting her. The spectral, half-compounded, aqueous light which pervaded the open mead impressed them with a feeling of isolation, as if they were Adam and Eve. (p. 186)

In a curious way this is Paradise, with the inverted twist that Eve has already been forced to eat of the tree of knowledge in the Chase. This suggestion is part of Hardy's irony, the emphasis being on the words 'as if'. The 'world' associations are powerful, for Hardy has succeeded in conveying the intensity of place and space.

The mood of foreground/background is varied by Hardy. Symbolically, poetically, he makes scenes resonant with associations, as above, giving them structural relevance, sympathetic and aesthetic power. Consider this:

Or perhaps the summer fog was more general, and the meadows lay like a white sea, out of which the scattered trees rose like dangerous rocks. Birds would soar through it into the upper radiance, and hang on the wing sunning themselves, or alight on the wet rails subdividing the mead, which now shone like glass rods. (p. 188)

The mixed, vibrant poetics of this are as visually and symbolically suggestive as Tess herself. The fog and rocks are in her past, present and future, but she is in the upper radiance of this place of love. Hardy also gives his foreground a different perspective, that of the orthodox outsider like Mr Clare: 'To the aesthetic, sensuous, pagan pleasure in natural life and lush womanhood which his son Angel had lately been experiencing in Var Vale, his temper would have been antipathetic in a high degree . . .' (p. 218). His sons might well have employed Hardy's deliberately pastoral language to describe Angel's reactions: 'A prig would have said that he had lost culture, and a prude that he had become coarse. Such was the contagion of domiciliary fellowship with the Talbothays nymphs and swains' (p. 219).

Talbothays is both rustic idyll and seasonal cyclic reality. Hardy's treatment considers both consciousness and perspective. Summer gives way to autumn and then winter, and Talbothays wears a different face. Here is a perspective in early November which marks the killing passage of time and its consonance with mood:

Looking over the damp sod in the direction of the sun, a glistening ripple of gossamer webs was visible to their eyes under the luminary, like the track of moonlight on the sea. Gnats, knowing nothing of their brief glorification, wandered across the shimmer of the pathway, irradiated as if they bore fire within them, then passed out of its line and were quite extinct. (p. 266)

This is before Tess has decided whether or not to marry Angel, but the tone is ominous. Nature's changes are men's and women's changes too, and the movements in seasonal employment occur accordingly. The dairyman will not need Tess's labour during the winter months, something that causes her anguish and in a way forces decision upon her. When they leave to go to the nearest town on Christmas Eve Tess is exposed to insult: it is as if she has stepped out of the impenetrable world of the dairy's security and back into the real world of suffering she knows so well. Yet it is the dairy which witnesses the greatest indicator of change, and not just in the weather, for the cock crows twice, the second time 'straight towards Clare' (p. 282). Much later Tess and the reunited dairymaids pay memory visits to Talbothays in nostalgia but before that Tess pays one in person. Her confession has brought about much more than a weather change.

The Wellbridge 'honeymoon' is a register of location but much more of mood, since it is packed with the incidents of emotional disintegration before the brief return just mentioned, when 'Tess went and bade all her favourite cows goodbye, touching each one of them with her hand . . .' (p. 323) This goodbye marks the beginning of Tess's journeys again, the first one 'home', the second to Flintcomb-Ash, which is seen in contrast to Talbothays seasonally and emotionally. Marlott cannot keep Tess, and when she arrives she sees that already her marriage has put her out of the family; as she surveys the rearranged beds she realizes 'There was no place here for her now' (p. 329). But while she is there Hardy uses an ironic counterpoise, for Clare returns to Wellbridge, finds the holly and, meeting Izz, proposes that she accompany him to Brazil, and quickly retracts. Here, each background acts as a hinge of separation in past and present, with the might-have-been in Angel's mind, as it always is in Tess's: 'That evening he was within a featherweight's turn of abandoning his road to the nearest station, and driving across that elevated dorsal line of South Wessex which divided him from his Tess's home' (p. 345). He doesn't, and their separate locations nearly kill them, physically in his case, emotionally in hers.

After eight months or so in Port Bredy Tess sets out for Chalk-Newton. This journey is as fraught as the others, and after a night spent in a wood she kills the wounded birds. She joins Marian at Flintcomb-Ash, but not before she has experienced a terrible sense of desolation, seen when she shelters against the house-wall at the entrance to the village. She is warmed by the bricks, and 'The wall seemed to be the only friend she had' (p. 356). Hardy injects social and moral commentary on her plight: female field-labour is the lowest level of occupation. Flintcomb-Ash is Tess's lowest ebb. The parallel with Talbothays is in the companionship: the contrast is in the season and place, with Tess's state mirrored in labour, terrain and mood. She looks back in anguish, but first of all she has to experience the 'starve-acre' place in its expanse of solitude. Here the description of place is atmospheric; more, the reality is stark:

The upper half of each turnip had been eaten off by the live-stock, and it was the business of the two women to grub up the lower or earthy half of the root with a hooked fork called a hacker, that it might be eaten also. Each leaf of the vegetable having already been consumed, the whole field was in colour a desolate drab; it was a complexion without features, as if a face, from chin to brow, should be only an expanse of skin. The sky wore, in another colour, the same likeness; a white vacuity of countenance with the lineaments gone. So these two upper and nether visages confronted each other all day long, the white face looking down on the brown face, and the brown face looking up at the white face, without anything standing between them but the two girls crawling over the surface of the former like flies. (p. 360)

The observant reader will have noticed that parts of this passage mirror Tess, for example in the reduction of her beauty when she snips off her eyebrows, the blankness of her life, the constant confrontation of the past and the present in her mind, the echo of the simple fly analogy employed when she overlooked Talbothays 'like a fly on a billiard-table of indefinite length' (p. 159). The overall effect is to pit man – here woman – against the vastness of the location – the world. Description, realism and symbol, as so often in Hardy, merge; place is the index to situation, the corollary of mood. The oppressive wetness the women experience is fact, as are the strange birds already noticed who can tell no travellers' tales. Their journey, like Tess's and Marian's, is one of displacement, their natural silence in their temporary terrain is as eloquent of experience as the loquacity of Tess and Marian reunited with the glow of the past to give them speech. Marian's greeting of Tess transcends present place in its emotional identification – '"Tess – Mrs Clare – the dear wife of dear he!"' (p. 357). There follows of course the journey to Emminster in hope and the return to Flintcomb-Ash in despair, the encounter on that return with Alec bringing back the past with a vengeance. Background as the permanence, with journeys taken across it as ephemeral as the lives involved, constitute Hardy's insistent commentary. Life is a journey or pilgrimage, and Tess's life is changed by the journeys she makes. In the novel the interlocking of background and fate is inevitable. Hardy's localization is specific with intent, as he makes clear from the General Preface to the Wessex Edition in 1912 where he wrote 'the description of these backgrounds has been done from the real – that is to say, has something real for its basis, however illusively treated' (p. 493).

With the arrival of the threshing-machine at Flintcomb-Ash comes the arrival of change. The permanence of the landscape will see changes other than the human ones. In his Introduction to the Penguin edition

A. Alvarez draws attention to the function of Hardy's description and identifiable patterns when he says 'the landscape is continually brought to life, not for its own sake but, like a sounding-board, in order to deepen and intensify whatever it is that Tess is experiencing' (p. 11). This is true, but there is, as commonly in Hardy, historical and social awareness too. Tess is the victim of her time as well as of Alec and Angel. The backgrounds don't alter her situation of deprivation, of movement, of displacement, of pleasant or sparse employment. They are real and symbolic, and with the irony which encompasses his study of Tess Hardy uses journeys and locations right through to the end of the novel. The contrast between Sandbourne and Stonehenge, for instance, the spacious urban watering-place and the isolated plain, symbolizes Tess as victim, as sacrifice. Her final journey in so many is yet to be taken, but at Stonehenge the weariness of emotional and physical travel is apparent. As she says to Angel, '"It is as it should be . . . Angel, I am almost glad – yes, glad!, that the journeying is over."' (p. 487)

9. Conclusion

The aim of any critical study is to send the reader back to the text being discussed; to suggest insights, interpretations, evaluations which that reader may question or challenge, part-accept or part-reject, in the course of personal, imaginative and disciplined reading. Hardy's career as a writer of fiction reaches its highest level in *Tess*. The analysis of narrative structures which occupies the main body of this study shows how careful, how continually committed, how sophisticated are his revisions (or restorations) and his artistic awareness. *Tess* evolves naturally out of his previous practice and his moral and philosophical predilections. But because of the centrality of the heroine, and the author's and reader's sympathetic identification with her, *Tess* is sustained at a higher level of immediacy, of full participation, than his previous novels. In *The Mayor of Casterbridge* (1886) and *The Woodlanders* (1887) the themes and concerns of *Tess* – tradition, the past and the present, fate, for example – are there. They are sensitively and imaginatively orchestrated, as indeed they are in the novel which follows *Tess*, *Jude the Obscure* (1895). All three are major novels, but the artistic complexity and completeness of *Tess* somehow conveys an elevation of the spirit despite the fatalistic content. The tragedy is at once local and universal. It is a *lived* novel, warm with life in humanity and nature, but carrying death at the centre of life. I think its continuing effect on readers of all generations derives from the intensity of this felt life, the perfection of the real and symbolic in the single human and artistic frame, which moves and disturbs at the same time. In 1883 Hardy wrote an essay called 'The Dorsetshire Labourer' which was published in *Longman's Magazine* in July of that year. He is operating in his own area, that of *Tess*, and says, among other things, that 'the community is assumed to be a uniform collection of concrete Hodges': *Tess* is a vibrant demonstration of individual difference. He talks of their language as being a mixture of 'the printed tongue' of the National School and the 'unwritten, dying, Wessex English that they had learnt of their parents'. This, certainly, is Tess. He writes of 'The Movement on Lady Day' and observes

The goods are built up on the waggon to a well-nigh unvarying pattern, which is probably as peculiar to the country labourer as the hexagon to the bee. The dresser, with its finger-marks and domestic evidence thick upon it . . . like some

114

Ark of the Covenant ... the looking-glass, usually held in the lap of the eldest girl.

This is seen with fictive poignancy in Chapter LII of *Tess* (pp. 443–4). In the same essay he wrote:

Women's labour, too, is highly in request, for a woman who, like a boy, fills the place of a man at half the wages, can be better depended on for steadiness ... In winter and spring a farmwoman's occupation is often 'turnip-hacking' – that is, picking out from the land the stumps of turnips which have been eaten off by the sheep – or feeding the threshing-machine, clearing away straw from the same, and standing on the rick to hand forward the sheaves ... Not a woman in the county but hates the threshing-machine. The dust, the din, the sustained exertion demanded to keep up with the steam tyrant, are distasteful to all women but the coarsest ... some years ago a woman had frequently to stand just above the whizzing wire drum and feed from morning to night – a performance for which she was quite unfitted ...

I give this in full, for no student of *Tess* can be unaware of its relevance. To appropriate one of the themes of the novel, here is Hardy's observed past feeding into his narrative. *Tess* is not documentary, but it is instinct with reality, of the way life was lived and the conditions and practices that made it what it was. But there is a verisimilitude which transcends the facts of place. It is the imaginative, sympathetic, humanitarian contemplation of humanity in adversity, with the corollary of courage to speak out against hypocrisy and injustice.

Selected Bibliography

This is here divided into Hardy's works, critical or scholarly appraisals which relate directly to *Tess of the d'Urbervilles*, and general and biographical studies.

1. Students and readers of *Tess* might refer to four or five other novels where the role of the heroine has some kinship with that of Tess, or contrasts with it in terms of Hardy's presentation and attitude. Of major interest here are:

> *Far from the Madding Crowd* (1874)
> *The Return of the Native* (1878)
> *The Mayor of Casterbridge* (1886)
> *The Woodlanders* (1887)
> *Jude the Obscure* (1895)

These are readily available in modern annotated editions (for example, Penguin Classics). Modern criticism (see Widdowson, Taylor below) would argue that other novels are equally deserving of close study, for instance:

> *A Pair of Blue Eyes* (1873)
> *The Hand of Ethelberta* (1876)
> *Two on a Tower* (1882)

Some of Hardy's *Wessex Tales* and his other stories are rewarding not only in reflecting his concerns but also his mastery of the shorter forms of fiction. The poetry, which has scarcely been mentioned in this Critical Study, is essential reading for anyone interested in Hardy and his development. Poetry was his first love, and after abandoning fiction (following the reception of *Jude the Obscure*) he returned increasingly to it, particularly after the death of his first wife in November 1912. *The Complete Poems* (ed. James Gibson, Macmillan, 1976) and the same editor's Variorum Edition (1978) are invaluable, and there are many selections in print. Hardy's range is considerable, and many of his themes resonate with or echo those found in *Tess*. Jean Brooks (see below) rightly points out that 'Beyond the Last Lamp', 'Tess's Lament', 'Proud Songsters' (see pp. 80 and 108–9 of this Critical Study) connect with *Tess*, as well as 'A Light Snow-Fall after Frost'. To these I would add a number, including 'Her Immortality', 'In a Ewe-Leaze near Weatherbury', 'The Well-Beloved', 'The Seasons of the Year', 'The Farm-Woman's Winter', The Ghost of the Past', 'Lost Love', 'In Death Divided' and many others.

2. For a detailed analytical investigation, see J. T. Laird, *The Shaping of 'Tess of the d'Urbervilles'* (Oxford, 1975), and the Introduction to *Tess of the d'Urbervilles*, edited by Juliet Grindle and Simon Gatrell (Clarendon Press, Oxford, 1983). The particular strengths of this edition are the general introduction, which covers writing, publication, and revisions, while the editorial introduction describes the main texts and establishes the procedure for presenting the variant readings. In addition, the complete text of 'Saturday Night in Arcady' and 'The Midnight Baptism' is included. These are both referred to in some detail in my introduction.

James Gibson's *Tess of the D'Urbervilles* (Macmillan, 1986) is an invaluable study of the novel. Of great help to the student of Hardy are the following, which all contain valuable material on *Tess of the d'Urbervilles*:

Cox, R. G. ed., *Thomas Hardy: The Critical Heritage* (Macmillan, 1970)
   Excellent introduction. Reviews of *Tess* are referred to on pp. 178–248.
Draper, R. P. ed., *Hardy: The Tragic Novels* (Macmillan, Casebook Series, 1975)
   This has comments by Hardy on *Tess* and extracts from his 'The Dorsetshire Labourer' and 'Candour in Fiction'. The section on *Tess* itself has extracts from two important books on Hardy:
   Douglas Brown's *Thomas Hardy* (Longman, 1954) and David Lodge's *The Language of Fiction* (Routledge & Kegan Paul, 1966) – the latter contains Tony Tanner's exemplary essay 'Colour and Movement in *Tess of the d'Urbervilles*' (*Critical Quarterly*, 10, Autumn 1968.

3. The following studies of Hardy, as well as biographies and his collected letters – will repay attention:

Bayley, John, *An Essay on Hardy* (Cambridge, 1978)
Boumelha, Penny, *Thomas Hardy and Women: Sexual Ideology and Narrative Form* (Harvester, 1984)
Brooks, Jean, *Thomas Hardy: The Poetic Structure* (Elek Books, 1971)

Critical Studies: Tess of the d'Urbervilles

Casagrande, Peter, *Unity in Hardy's Novels: 'Repetitive Symmetries'* (Macmillan, 1982)

Cecil, David, *Hardy the Novelist* (Constable, 1943)

Gittings, Robert, *Young Thomas Hardy* (Heinemann, 1975; Penguin, Penguin Literary Biographies, 1978)

— *The Older Hardy* (Heinemann, 1978; Penguin, Penguin Literary Biographies, 1980)

Gregor, Ian, *The Great Web: The Form of Hardy's Major Fiction* (Faber, 1974)

Hardy, Florence Emily, *The Life of Thomas Hardy* (Macmillan, 1975) This is effectively Hardy's autobiography, and was issued as *The Early Life of Thomas Hardy* (1928) and *The Later Years of Thomas Hardy* (1930).

Hardy, Thomas, *The Collected Letters of Thomas Hardy*, ed. R. L. Purdy and Michael Millgate (Oxford, 1978–88)

Ingham, Patricia, *Thomas Hardy* (Harvester, 1989) This contains a very useful summary of feminist writings on Hardy (pp. 1–8) and is particularly perceptive on the later novels.

Kramer, Dale, *Thomas Hardy: The Forms of Tragedy* (Macmillan, 1975)

Kramer, Dale, ed., *Critical Approaches to the Fiction of Thomas Hardy*, (Macmillan, 1979)

Lawrence, D. H., 'Study of Thomas Hardy' (1914), in *Phoenix*, (Heinemann, 1961)

Miller, J. Hillis, *Thomas Hardy, Distance and Desire* (Oxford, 1970)

Millgate, Michael, *Thomas Hardy: A Biography* (Oxford, 1982) Scholarly, carefully researched, with the works in mind throughout.

Pinion, F. B., *A Hardy Companion* (Macmillan, 1968)

Purdy, R. L., *Thomas Hardy: A Bibliographical Study* (Oxford, 1954)

Taylor, Richard H., *The Neglected Hardy: Thomas Hardy's Lesser Novels* (Macmillan, 1982)

Weber, Carl, *Hardy of Wessex* (1940; Routledge & Kegan Paul, 1965)

Widdowson, Peter, *Hardy in History: A Study in Literary Sociology* (Routledge, 1989)

Williams, Merrin, *Thomas Hardy and Rural England* (Macmillan, 1972)

NOTE: Roman Polanski's film of *Tess of the d'Urbervilles* was released in France (where it was filmed) in 1979 and elsewhere in 1981. For a superb discussion of it see Widdowson (above), pp. 115–26.